House Spe

Simon MacDonald

House Specials

1st Edition

Copyright © 2022 Simon MacDonald

All rights reserved

Published by Quiraang Press

To Neil

Bon Appetite!

Simon MacDonald

Contents

Introduction	5
Meat	6
Boeuf Bourguignon	7
Black Pudding Meatballs	10
Confit Duck Legs	13
Grilled Marinated Lamb Chops	15
Lamb and Dhal Curry	17
Pig Cheeks Braised in Marsala	19
Quail Scotch Eggs	21
Quiche Lorraine	23
Lamb Kofta	26
Sardinian Lamb	28
Sicilian Lamb Meatballs	30
Small Cottage Pie	32
Swedish Meatballs	35
Poultry	38
Buttermilk Fried Chicken	39
Chicken Breasts Stuffed and Wrapped in Prosciutto	41
Chicken and Mushroom Casserole	43
Chicken Escalopes	45
Chicken Marsala	47
Chicken and Sweet Potato Korma	49
Chicken Parmigiana	51
Chicken Satay	53
Chicken Tenders	55
Italian Style Buffalo Wings	57
Hendo's Buffalo Wings	58
Fish	60

Fish Cakes — 61
Fish Pie — 63
Haddock Goujons with a Nut and Herb Crumb — 65
Prawn Cocktail — 66
Salmon with Ginger — 68
Tiger Prawn Pasta Sauce — 69

Vegetables — 72

Barley, Butternut Squash, and Spinach Risotto — 73
Bombay Potatoes — 75
Boulangère Potatoes — 77
Dhal — 78
Spiced Green Lentils — 80
Nut Roast — 82
Perfect Mushrooms on Toast — 84
Pea Soup — 85
Risotto Primavera — 87
Stuffed Field Mushrooms — 90
Stuffed Butternut Squash — 92

Baking and Desserts — 94

Bakewell Tart — 95
Brack — 97
Carrot and Walnut Muffins — 99
Christmas Cake — 100
Granola — 103
Panna Cotta — 105
Pear Frangipane Tart — 107
Shortbread — 109
Soda Bread — 110
Sticky Toffee Pudding — 111
Tiramisu — 113

Walnut and Sultana Bread	115
Sides, Marinades and Sauces	117
Nut and Herb Crumb for Fish or Chicken	118
House Gravy Recipe	119
Greek Style Marinade	121
Italian Style Marinade	122
Middle East Style Marinade	123
Inferno Sauce	124
Pesto	126
Sweet Chilli Sauce	127
Tempura	128
Velveting	130
Yorkshire pudding	132
Spices and Seasonings	133
Baharat	134
Garam Masala	135
Ginger and Garlic Paste	136
Ras el Hanout	137
Korma Paste	138
Vegetable Seasoning	139
Notes and Conversion Tables	140

Introduction

I am a cook not a chef. I became a cook because I like food - good food.

My upbringing was in the Scottish Highlands where the diet was plain, but plentiful. In my late teens I got a job in London, and this was quite a culture shock for me. I very soon discovered that London had many places to eat which had good, inexpensive food. I had never seen so many restaurants and cafés serving such a variety of cuisines and dishes. This meant I was able to try out food that I had never tasted, and even dishes I had never known about.

Some people regard eating as merely fuelling the body, but in my opinion, food is one of the great pleasures in life. Food does not need to be complicated or expensive to be good, and should be enjoyed wherever, and whenever, possible. So, to enjoy good food, I taught myself to cook. I also discovered the pleasure of cooking for others, sharing in their enjoyment of something I had created.

The recipes in this book are a few of my favourite dishes. They are dishes that I eat regularly. Some are simple, others a little more complicated. However, they all have one thing in common - they are tasty!

I hope you enjoy them as much as I do.

Bon appetite!

Simon MacDonald

Meat

Boeuf Bourguignon

A traditional French style beef stew cooked with red wine carrots, mushrooms, bacon and small shallots. Utterly delicious.

Serves 6

Ingredients

- 1kg good-quality shin beef, trimmed of excess fat and sinew.
- 4–5 tbsp olive oil
- 100g streaky bacon, cut into 2cm pieces
- 1 large banana shallot, finely chopped
- 2 garlic cloves, crushed
- 300ml red wine
- 2 tbsp tomato purée
- 400ml strong beef stock
- 2 large bay leaves
- 3 bushy sprigs fresh thyme
- 25g butter
- 450g small shallots
- 300g chestnut mushrooms, wiped and halved or quartered if large.
- 1 stick of celery, finely diced
- 2 carrots peeled and cut I'm medium size chunks.
- 4 tbsp plain flour
- sea salt and freshly ground black pepper
- chopped fresh parsley, to garnish
- cornflour - optional

Method

1. Heat the oven to 170°C/150°C fan.
2. Cut the shin beef into chunky pieces, each around 4–5cm. Trim off any really hard fat or sinew.
3. Put the flour in a bowl and season well with salt and pepper. Add the chunks of beef and mix well so each chunk has an even coat of flour.
4. Heat two tablespoons of the oil in a large frying pan. Shake off any excess flour and fry the beef in three batches over a medium–high heat until nicely browned on all sides, turning every now and then and adding more oil if necessary. As soon as the beef is browned, transfer to a large flameproof casserole.
5. Pour a little more oil into the pan in which the beef was browned and fry the bacon for 2–3 minutes, or until the fat crisps and browns. Scatter the bacon over the meat. Add a touch more oil to the frying pan and fry the chopped onion over a low heat for 5–6 minutes, stirring often until softened. Stir the garlic into the pan and cook for 1 minute more.
6. Deglaze the pan with a little red wine.
7. Add the onion and garlic to the pan with the meat and pour over the remaining wine, and stock. Stir in the tomato purée.
8. Add the herbs, celery and carrot, and bring to a simmer. Stir well, cover with a lid and transfer to the oven. Cook for 2 hours, or until the beef is almost completely tender.
9. While the beef is cooking, peel the button onions. Put the onions in a heatproof bowl and cover with just-boiled water. Leave to stand for five minutes and then drain. When the onions are cool enough to handle, trim off the root close to the end so they don't fall apart and peel off the skin.
10. A few minutes before the beef is ready, melt half of the butter in a large non-stick frying pan with a touch of oil

and fry the onions over a medium heat for about 5 minutes, or until golden brown on all sides. Tip into a bowl.

11. Remove the casserole from the oven, and add the onions, and mushrooms. Return to the oven and cook for 45 minutes more, or until the beef is meltingly tender and the sauce is thick. The sauce should coat the back of a spoon – if it remains fairly thin, simply add a little cornflour, blended with a little cold water and simmer for a couple of minutes on the hob.

12. To serve, remove the thyme stalks. Sprinkle the casserole with parsley and serve.

Black Pudding Meatballs

A twist on the classic recipe for meatballs. Adding black pudding gives a rich and intense flavour that makes these meatballs extremely scrumptious.

Serves 4

Ingredients

For the meatballs

- 500g minced beef
- 250g black pudding
- 2 garlic cloves, grated
- 3 tbsp finely chopped parsley, plus extra to serve
- 2 tbsp finely chopped chives, plus extra to serve
- 1 tsp dried thyme
- 2 tbsp porridge oats
- 2 large free-range eggs
- 2 tsp sea salt
- a large pinch of black pepper

For the tomato sauce

- 3 tbsp olive oil
- 2 banana shallots, roughly chopped
- 1 tsp dried thyme
- 3 tbsp finely chopped flat-leaf parsley
- 400g tin chopped tomatoes
- 2 garlic cloves, grated
- 1 tbsp tomato purée
- 2 tsp Henderson's Relish

- 2 tsp sea salt

Method

1. Take the minced beef and black pudding out of the fridge so they lose their chill while you get on with the sauce. Pour 400ml cold water into a measuring jug and put it by the hob.
2. To make the sauce, warm the oil in a large heavy-based casserole then add the onion and cook over a medium heat, stirring every now and then, for about 5 minutes or until beginning to soften and turn golden in parts.
3. When the banana shallots are ready, stir in the dried thyme, parsley and garlic. Add the tomatoes, then swill out the empty tin with the water in your jug and pour it into the pan. Stir in the tomato puree, Henderson's Relish and salt and then turn up the heat to bring to the boil. Once boiling, turn down the heat and simmer for 10 minutes.
4. Meanwhile, make the meatballs. Loosen the mince with your fingers as you drop it into a large bowl. Add the black pudding, crumbling it in by hand. Add the garlic, parsley, chives, dried thyme, salt, pepper and chilli flakes, then sprinkle over the oats and crack in the eggs. Mix this all together with your hands, making sure it's evenly incorporated.
5. Tear off walnut-sized lumps of the mixture and roll them between your palms to make meatballs, placing them on a lined baking sheet or large chopping board as you go. You should end up making about 40.
6. Drop the meatballs into the sauce in concentric circles, easing them in gently. Try to get the meatballs covered by the sauce and then bring to a bubble. Put on the lid, turn the heat down a bit, and let it simmer for 15 minutes.
7. Take off the lid and give the pan a very gentle stir, then leave without a lid for another 15 minutes, simmering a

little less now, by which time the meatballs should be cooked through.

8. Check the sauce for seasoning, then leave off the heat for 5–10 minutes. Ladle into bowls, sprinkle with chives and parsley and eat with bread and butter or a buttery bowl of colcannon.

Confit Duck Legs

Confit duck legs are slow-cooked in duck fat until the meat is meltingly tender, then the skin crisped to golden perfection. A classic French dish.

Serves 4

Ingredients

- 4 duck legs
- 30g coarse sea salt
- 1 tbsp black peppercorns, crushed
- 4 garlic cloves, peeled and finely grated
- 2 bay leaves, finely sliced
- 4 sprigs thyme
- 800g duck fat, melted

Method

1. Mix together the sea salt, crushed pepper, garlic, thyme and bay leaves. Spread one third on a tray.
2. Lay the duck legs on the tray - flesh side upwards - and distribute the remaining salt mix evenly over the flesh side. Cover with cling film and marinate overnight (at least 12 hours).
3. Heat the oven to 120°C/100°C fan. Brush off the marinade and pat dry with kitchen cloth. Place the duck legs skin side down in a roasting pan. Cover with the melted duck fat, place on the stove and bring the temperature to 100°C/85°C fan. Place in the oven and cook for 2¼ hours until the duck legs are very tender.

4. Using a food temperature probe, check the duck fat doesn't go any higher than 90ºC, just under simmering point.
5. Once cooked, put the legs in a bowl and leave to cool in the fat and store in the fridge for 2-3 days, which will improve the flavour.
6. To serve, remove the confit duck legs from their fat, and heat the oven to 200°C/180°C fan. Put an ovenproof frying pan on the stove until it is hot. Add the duck legs, skin-side down, and cook for 4 minutes. Turn the legs and transfer the pan to the oven for 30 minutes, until crisp.

Grilled Marinated Lamb Chops

These lamb chops will probably be the best you have ever tasted. Succulent, tender, and flavourful!

Serves 2

Ingredients

- handful of fresh herbs, chopped finely (oregano, rosemary, thyme, winter savoury, parsley...) or 1 tsp each of dried oregano and mixed herbs.
- 2 large cloves garlic, peeled and finely grated
- 4 tbsp olive oil
- 1 tsp balsamic vinegar
- 1 tsp honey
- optional: 1 clove of black garlic, finely grated
- ¼ tsp sea salt
- ¼ tsp freshly ground black pepper
- 8 lamb chops

Method

1. Using paper towels, pat dry chops and discard any bone fragments.
2. Mix all of the ingredients together in a small jug or bowl.
3. Arrange lamb chops in a large baking dish or on a large plate, and pour the marinade all over the lamb, rubbing it into the meat. Cover and marinate for half an hour, or for a deeper flavour, marinate overnight in the refrigerator, turning the chops from time to time (before cooking, let lamb chops sit at room temperature for 30 minutes).
4. Heat the grill to a high heat. Grill lamb for 3-4 minutes each side, depending on thickness until done to your

liking. (Usually, at 3 minutes per side they are medium, and at 4 minutes they are medium-well.)
5. Let rest for 5 minutes before serving. Sprinkle with a little extra dried oregano for added flavour and a little extra lemon juice (optional).

Lamb and Dhal Curry

Succulent spicy lamb backed up by the earthy flavours of chana dhal.

Serves 4

Ingredients

- 2 tsp **ginger and garlic paste** (see recipe on page 136)
- 1 large onion, peeled, halved, and thinly sliced
- 150g chana dhal, soaked over-night (Tip: pour over boiling water and leaving for 30 minutes has the same effect)
- 1 small Bird's eye chili, de-seeded and chopped (add more if you wish!)
- 1 medium, mild green chili, de-seeded and chopped
- 2 tbsp tomato purée
- 750g shoulder of lamb, excess fat removed, chopped to 2.5cm dice
- 500ml lamb stock
- 2 tbsp ground nut oil,
- sea salt

Spices

- 1 tsp ground fenugreek
- 2 tsp ground coriander
- 2 tsp ground cumin
- 1 tsp ground turmeric
- 2 cloves
- 3 green cardamoms, bruised
- ½ tsp ground black pepper

- 1 tsp tamarind paste
- 10 curry leaves

Method

1. Fry onions very slowly over a low heat with about 1 tbsp oil, until very soft and slightly browned - about 20 minutes. Do not burn them. Remove into a bowl.
2. Wipe out the pan and heat 1 tbsp oil. Add the fenugreek, cumin, coriander, and turmeric to the oil and heat over a low heat for 2-3 minutes to cook the spices.
3. Add the onions and ginger and garlic paste to the spices and mix well.
4. Add the meat and coat it well with the spice/onion/paste mix.
5. Add the stock and bring to a simmer.
6. Add all the remaining ingredients.
7. Put into a low/medium oven, 160°C/150°C fan for about 1½ hours.
8. Check and stir every 20 minutes. Add a little water if it looks to be burning. It should end up medium thick sauce.
9. When the sauce is thick and the meat very tender add salt to taste.

Pig Cheeks Braised in Marsala

Pig cheeks are a tender and flavour-some cut of meat that is not widely used. However, once you have eaten these unctuous little nuggets of deliciousness, you will want to cook them regularly. The secret is in slow cooking, at a low temperature. Most good butchers will either have them or order them for you. The recipe is very simple, so go on, and treat yourself!

Serves 4

Ingredients

- 12 pig cheeks
- 2 celery sticks, chopped in 1cm chunks
- 3 carrots, chopped in 1cm chunks
- 1 banana shallot chopped in 1cm chunks
- 6 garlic cloves, peeled and crushed
- a sprig of thyme, leaves only
- 1 bay leaf
- 300ml Marsala or Madeira wine
- 400ml chicken stock
- 40g plain flour
- 1 tsp sea salt,
- ¼ tsp black pepper
- 3 tbsp groundnut oil

Method

1. Heat the oven to 150°C/130°C fan.
2. Heat a non-stick sauté pan and add 1 tablespoon of oil.

3. Place the vegetables, crushed garlic, bay leaf, and thyme in the bottom of an oven-proof casserole dish; the dish should be able to fit the pig cheeks in one layer.
4. Trim any excess fat and sinew from the pig cheeks.
5. Season the flour with the sea salt and black pepper, and coat four of the pig cheeks in the seasoned flour.
6. Brown the pig cheeks in the oil - about 2 minutes a side and put them on top of the vegetables in the casserole dish.
7. Continue coating and browning the pig cheeks in batches of four, adding more oil if required, and add them to the casserole dish so that you have one layer of meat on top of the vegetables.
8. Now de-glaze the sauté pan with the wine and add the wine and juices to the casserole dish.
9. Pour the chicken stock into the casserole dish, so that the pig cheeks are just showing above the surface of the liquid.
10. Crumple up a sheet of baking paper and wet it under a tap. Now unfold the paper and use it to cover the meat, tucking it down at the sides.
11. Place the dish in the heated oven and cook for 1 hour.
12. Turn over each pig cheek, cover again and cook for another 1 hour and 20 minutes. The pig cheeks should now be tender and nicely brown.
13. Carefully remove the pig cheeks and vegetables and set aside, and keep warm.
14. Strain the gravy into a small saucepan, bring to the boil, and reduce the volume by half.
15. Return the vegetables and meat to the casserole and pour the reduced sauce over them. Cover again and re-heat in the oven for ten minutes.
16. Serve with buttery mashed potatoes and a green vegetable.

Quail Scotch Eggs

These little beauties are just like the traditional scotch egg, but smaller and even tastier. Everybody loves them, so make sure you make enough.

Serves 4

Ingredients

- 6 Cumberland sausages - about 300g
- ½ tsp sweet paprika
- ½ tsp dried oregano
- ½ tsp dried sage
- ½ tsp freshly grated nutmeg
- 100g of plain flour
- 2 large free-range hens eggs
- 120g panko breadcrumbs
- 12 free-range quail's eggs
- vegetable oil, about 2 litres
- sea salt and freshly ground black pepper

Method

1. Put the kettle on to boil.
2. Tear open the sausages and squeeze the meat into a bowl. Season with the paprika, the herbs, nutmeg and a little sea salt and black pepper, then use a fork to mash it all up.
3. Beat the hens eggs in a bowl. Put the flour and breadcrumbs into 2 separate bowls, so you have 3 bowls in total.

4. Carefully put the quail's eggs into a small pan. Once the kettle boils, pour in the boiling water straight away and cook for 2 minutes, no longer.

5. Move the pan to the sink and run cold water over the eggs for 2 to 3 minutes. Tap, roll the eggs – very gently – and peel the shells off them. Do it under running water if it helps. You'll get quicker at peeling them as you go.

6. Take a marble-sized piece of sausage meat and flatten it out in the palm of your clean hand until it's about 6cm in diameter. Pop an egg into the middle, then carefully shape and mould the sausage meat up around the egg with your floured hands. You need to get into the routine of pulling up the sides, gently squeezing, moulding, patting and very gently squashing the meat around the egg.

7. Repeat with all 12 eggs, then coat them well with flour. Transfer them to the bowl of beaten egg and coat well, then roll them in the breadcrumbs. They'll be more robust to hold now, so pat and hug them into shape. When they're all done, put them into a container and pop them into the fridge until needed.

8. When you're ready to cook, put a deep casserole-type pan on a medium-high heat and fill it about 8cm deep with vegetable oil. Make sure you never fill a pan more than halfway up. Add a piece of potato to help you gauge the temperature – it's ready once the potato turns golden and floats (or when the oil reaches 180°C on a thermometer).

9. Carefully lower one Scotch egg into the pan. After about 4 minutes it should be golden and perfectly cooked through, so take it out of the pan and cut it in half to see if you should have cooked it for less or more time – once you know where you stand, you can cook the rest, in batches of 6 or less.

10. Transfer the cooked Scotch eggs to a plate lined with kitchen paper to drain, and serve scattered with a pinch of salt, alongside a pot of English mustard and a cold beer.

Quiche Lorraine

Originally from Lorraine in France, this dish has always been a favourite of picnics and summer buffets. Serve with a green salad, and a chilled glass of white wine. Just the thing to get you in the mood for the coming summer.

Serves 4

Ingredients

The shortcrust pastry

- 200g plain flour, sifted
- 100g butter, chilled and cubed
- pinch of sea salt
- 1 medium egg, beaten

The filling

- 150g pancetta, cut into 1cm lardons
- 3 medium echalion shallots, peeled and finely chopped
- 2 whole eggs and 2 egg yolks
- 200ml crème fraiche plus 1 tbsp milk
- 1 tbsp chopped chives
- 50g cheddar cheese, grated
- 50g gruyère cheese, grated
- a pinch each of sea salt and white pepper

Tips

- Instead of pastry, use a layer of thinly sliced sweet potatoes.
- Instead of pancetta, you can use chopped cooked ham slices

Method

The shortcrust pastry

1. Put the flour, butter and a pinch of salt in a food processor and process briefly.
2. Add the beaten egg and continue to process. The mixture should be just moist enough to come together. If making the pastry by hand, rub the butter into the flour until it resembles breadcrumbs then, using your hands, add just enough egg to bring it together.
3. With your hands, flatten out the ball of dough until it is about 2cm thick, then wrap it in cling film, and leave in the fridge for at least 30 minutes before using it.
4. Heat the oven to 180°C/160°C fan.
5. Line a 20cm high-sided tart tin or dish with the shortcrust pastry, prick the sides and base of the pastry with a fork. Cover the base with a circle of baking parchment.
6. Fill the tin with baking beans and bake blind for 10-15 minutes.
7. Remove the beans and parchment for the last five minutes of baking for a golden crust.

The filling

1. Heat a non-stick sauté pan and cook the pancetta for 5-6 minutes, or until crisp. You should not need any extra oil as the pancetta will release enough fat to cook it.
2. Remove and drain on kitchen paper.
3. Sweat the shallots gently in the same fat for a further ten minutes, or until softened.
4. Meanwhile, whisk the two whole eggs and two egg yolks in a jug,
5. Add the crème fraiche and the milk along with the salt and pepper and mix together well.

6. Mix together the shallots and pancetta and spread this in a layer on the pastry.
7. Next sprinkle the cheeses in a second layer over the onion and pancetta.
8. Then sprinkle the chives over the top of the cheese.
9. Pour the filling into the pastry base, place the quiche dish on a tray, and return to the oven to bake for 30-40 minutes, or until the centre has set.
10. Serve warm, with a green salad.

Lamb Kofta

I love these koftas! They are best grilled on a charcoal barbecue, but a hot grill or griddle pan can be used instead.

Serves 4

Ingredients

- 500g lean lamb mince
- 1 tbsp fresh thyme leaves
- 1 tbsp chopped mint leaves
- 1 pinch chilli flakes
- 1 tsp ground cumin
- 2 tsp **ras el hanout** spice mix (see recipe on page 137)
- 2 tbsp of shelled pistachio nuts crushed up finely
- 2 cloves of garlic finely chopped
- ½ tsp Sea salt
- ¼ tsp freshly ground black pepper

Method

1. Soak some bamboo skewers in water for a couple of hours. This will stop them catching fire when you grill them.
2. Mix all the ingredients together, ensuring that everything is evenly mixed, and leave in the fridge for a couple of hours to let the flavour develop.
3. With wet hands divide the mixture into 12 'sausages' (roughly 40g each) and insert a bamboo skewer into each one.

4. These are best cooked on a charcoal barbeque, but a hot grill or griddle pan can be used instead. Cook until golden brown on all sides

Sardinian Lamb

Lamb and fennel are a very popular combination in Sardinia and makes a wonderfully aromatic dish.

Serves 4

Ingredients

- 500g lamb (neck fillet or shoulder), cut into 6cm chunks, removing any excess fatty bits.
- 1 tbsp plain flour
- ½ tbsp fennel seeds, crushed
- pinch saffron, ground up
- 4 tbsp olive oil
- 2 banana shallots, finely chopped
- 3 garlic cloves, finely chopped
- 1 tbsp tomato puree
- 100ml dry vermouth
- 300ml lamb stock
- 2 large tomatoes, skinned and roughly chopped
- bouquet garni, made from 2 bay leaves, sprig of parsley, sprig of rosemary
- 2 fennel bulbs
- 1 tsp honey
- salt and freshly ground black pepper

To serve

- small bunch fresh parsley, finely chopped
- small bunch fresh basil, shredded

Method

1. Put the lamb in a large bowl. Season with salt and pepper, then sprinkle over the flour, fennel seeds and saffron. Turn over to coat.
2. Heat a tablespoon of the oil in a large casserole dish. Add the lamb and fry on all sides, making sure you get a good, deep brown crust. Do this in two batches if necessary – do not crowd the pan as this will stop them from browning properly.
3. Remove the lamb from the casserole and set aside. Add a little more oil if necessary and fry the shallots on a lower heat until soft and translucent. Add the garlic and cook for a further minute or two.
4. Turn up the heat and pour in the vermouth. Stir, scraping up any brown bits from the base of the pan. Return the lamb to the casserole, (and any remaining flour) then pour in enough stock to just cover the lamb. Add the chopped tomatoes, honey, tomato purée and the bouquet garni.
5. Heat the oven to 160°C/140°C fan.
6. Bring to the boil, then turn down the heat to a low simmer. Cover and cook for an hour in the oven.
7. Meanwhile, prepare the fennel bulbs. Trim the tops, cutting off any fronds and reserving for later. Trim the bare minimum from the bases, then cut each bulb in half lengthways. Cut each half into three wedges, also lengthways. You should find these hold together, although the outer layers may come away from the root. Heat the remaining olive oil in a large frying pan, then fry the fennel until caramelised round the edges. Set aside.
8. When the lamb has cooked for an hour, add the fennel. Continue to cook, for another hour, until the fennel is very tender, and the liquid has reduced down a little further. Taste for seasoning. Sprinkle with the parsley and basil.

Sicilian Lamb Meatballs

Succulent meatballs with raisins and pine nuts that make this dish distinctly Sicilian.

Serves 6

Ingredients

For the sauce

- 1 banana shallot finely chopped
- 1 clove garlic finely grated
- 1 tsp mixed herbs
- 1 tsp sugar
- 200ml tomato passata
- 200ml water
- 1 beef stock cube
- 100ml vermouth rosso or strong red wine

For the meatballs

- 500g lamb mince
- 30g pine nuts roughly chopped
- 30g chopped raisins soaked in a splash of brandy or red wine
- 50g finely grated Parmesan cheese
- 50g unseasoned breadcrumbs
- 2 eggs
- 2 large garlic cloves finely grated
- 2 finely chopped spring onions
- 1 tbsp chopped mint leaves
- 1 tsp oregano

- 1 tsp lemon juice
- 1 tsp kosher salt
- ½ tsp black pepper
- 3 tbsp olive oil

Method

1. Combine all the meatball ingredients in a bowl.
2. Form meatballs into uniform balls - about walnut size.
3. Heat the olive oil in a sauté pan and fry the meatballs in batches on a medium heat turning often to brown on all sides, about 10 minutes per batch. They don't have to be cooked all the way through, just browned.
4. Remove the meatballs to a dish.
5. Add the shallot to the pan and sauté gently until softened.
6. Pour in the vermouth and simmer for 1 minute, then add the garlic, passata and water. Crumble in the beef stock cube and stir well.
7. Return the meatballs to the pan and simmer for 25-30 minutes.

Small Cottage Pie

This is a delicious Cottage Pie that serves two people. Just increase the quantities for 4 or 6 people.

Serves 2

Ingredients

- 250g lean minced beef
- 1 banana shallot, chopped
- 1 celery stick finely diced
- 1 medium carrot diced
- 2 cloves garlic finely grated
- 1 tbsp tomato purée
- 600ml beef stock made with 2 beef stock cubes
- 2 tbsp Henderson's Relish or Worcestershire Sauce
- 1 tsp dried oregano
- ¼ tsp dried thyme
- 2 tbsp flour
- 1 tbsp olive oil
- 75ml vermouth rosso or strong red wine
- large pinch of sea salt
- freshly ground black pepper

Sweet potato topping

- 300g sweet potato
- 1 tbsp butter
- small pinch of sea salt
- freshly ground black pepper

- Optional: Grated cheese to add on top before cooking in the oven)

Method

1. Place a medium pan over a medium heat.
2. Heat the oil and gently soften the shallots.
3. Add the mince and the garlic, celery and carrots. Cook for 10 minutes until lightly coloured. Use a couple of wooden spoons to break up the meat as it cooks.
4. Add the flour and mix well.
5. Stir in the tomato purée, vermouth, beef stock, Henderson's Relish or Worcestershire sauce and herbs. Season with plenty of freshly ground black pepper. Bring to the boil, then reduce the heat, cover loosely and simmer gently for 20 minutes, stirring occasionally until the mince is tender. Take off the heat and check the seasoning.
6. Don't worry if it seems too wet, the extra gravy is sieved off to serve on the side.
7. Peel the sweet potatoes and cut them into thick slices. Put them in a boiling steamer and cook for 13-15 minutes or until the potatoes are very tender.
8. Drain and mash the potatoes with the butter, salt and black pepper.
9. Heat the oven to 200°C/180°C fan.
10. Pour the beef mixture through a coarse sieve into a bowl to catch the gravy. Tip the mixture from the sieve into a shallow ovenproof dish. Add a little more gravy if needed. Keep the remaining gravy to serve on the side.
11. Using a large spoon or spatula, top the mince with the mashed potatoes. Spoon the sweet potato mixture all around the edge of the dish before heading into the middle, then fluff up with a fork. Add the grated cheese if using.

12. Bake for 20 minutes until the topping is golden and the filling is bubbling.
13. If making this ahead of time, let the pie cool, then cover and put in the fridge. Cook from chilled in a heated oven at 210°C/190°C fan for 30-40 minutes or until the pie is piping hot throughout.

Swedish Meatballs

Swedish Meatballs have been made famous all over the world, by a well-known Scandinavian furniture company. These meat balls are delicious, beautifully complemented by the tangy and creamy sauce. You won't be able to stop eating them!

Serves 4

Ingredients

For the meatballs

- 1 tsp dried oregano
- 1 tsp dried marjoram
- 250g lean minced pork
- 250g lean minced beef or turkey thigh mince
- 1 large egg
- 100ml milk
- 60g dried breadcrumbs
- ½ tsp ground nutmeg
- 1 clove of garlic peeled and finely grated
- 1 tsp sea salt
- ½ tsp freshly ground black pepper
- 2 tbsp olive oil

For the sauce

- juice of ½ a lemon
- 400ml strong beef stock
- 1 tbsp plain flour
- 60ml double cream
- Lingonberry or cranberry jelly, to serve

Method

1. Place breadcrumbs in the bowl of a stand mixer fitted with a paddle attachment and add milk.
2. Let them sit until the bread has absorbed the milk, about 5 minutes.
3. Add the minced beef and pork, egg, salt, pepper, nutmeg, and herbs, and beat on medium speed until the mixture is light in colour and appears sticky - about 5 minutes.
4. Fill a medium bowl with water. Form the meat mixture into 2cm balls, wetting your hands in the bowl of water as necessary to keep the mixture from sticking, and place meatballs on a baking sheet.
5. Heat the 2 tablespoons of oil in a large sauté pan over medium heat.
6. Add half of the meatballs and fry, turning occasionally, until browned on all sides and cooked through, about 8 to 10 minutes.
7. Transfer to a clean serving dish and set aside. Repeat with remaining meatballs.
8. When all the meatballs have been cooked, sprinkle flour over the remaining oil in the pan and whisk, scraping up any browned bits, and cook for about 1 minute.
9. Slowly pour in beef stock, whisking as you do to smooth out any lumps.
10. Now stir in the lemon juice and cook until the mixture starts to boil and thicken.
11. Strain through a fine-mesh strainer into a medium heatproof bowl and discard the solids. Transfer the strained sauce back to the pan.
12. Reduce heat to low and whisk in the crème fraiche. Season with salt and pepper as needed.

13. Return meatballs to the pan until heated through.
14. Transfer meatballs and sauce to a serving dish and sprinkle with parsley.
15. Serve with mashed potatoes and Lingonberry, or cranberry jelly

Poultry

Buttermilk Fried Chicken

Crisp and flavoursome, this fried chicken is possibly one of the best you will ever taste.

Serves 4

Ingredients

- 2 tbsp sweet paprika
- 1 tbsp fennel seeds, crushed
- 8 free range chicken thigh fillets, trimmed
- 500ml buttermilk
- 300g plain flour
- 1 tbsp baking powder
- 2 tsp sea salt flakes, plus extra to serve
- ½ tsp cracked black pepper
- vegetable oil, for deep-frying

Method

1. Place the paprika and fennel seeds in a large bowl and mix to combine. Add the chicken and toss to coat. Add the buttermilk, mix to combine and refrigerate for 30 minutes.
2. Fill a large saucepan two-thirds full of oil and place over medium heat until the temperature reaches 180°C on a deep-frying thermometer.
3. While the oil is heating, place the flour, baking powder, salt and pepper on a large tray and toss to combine.

4. Remove the chicken from the buttermilk mixture, allowing any excess liquid to drip off. Place on the tray with the flour mixture and toss to coat evenly.
5. Deep-fry the chicken, in batches, for 5–6 minutes or until crisp, golden and cooked through. Drain on paper towel and keep warm. Sprinkle with extra salt to serve.

Chicken Breasts Stuffed and Wrapped in Prosciutto

This is one of our favourite chicken dishes. Chicken breasts with a succulent stuffing wrapped in prosciutto

Serves 2

Ingredients

- 2 medium chicken breasts
- 8 slices prosciutto ham

Stuffing mix

- 4 spring onions, white and green parts
- 4 large Medjool dates, stoned
- a small bunch of parsley leaves
- 1 tsp of fresh thyme leaves
- 2 or 3 cloves of garlic
- 10 pistachio nuts
- 10 cashew nuts
- 25g of finely grated Parmesan cheese
- 1 tbsp Olive oil
- Salt and pepper for seasoning

Method

1. Using a very sharp, narrow knife, carefully cut a 1 cm slit in the thick end of each breast. Carefully work the knife blade down the length of the breast to make a cavity. Make sure not to pierce the sides of the breast.
2. Put the stuffing ingredients into a food processor and pulse until you have a coarse paste.

3. Put half the stuffing mix into each breast, using a small spoon. You could also use an icing syringe with a long nozzle to fill them.
4. Lay out 4 slices of prosciutto, side by side, slightly overlapping on the long side.
5. Place a stuffed breast across the 4 slices at the top.
6. Turn over the breast once, bring the prosciutto slices with it. Now fold in the side slices, and finish rolling up. You should have nice neat wrapped breast.
7. Heat the oven to 200°C/180°C fan. Place the breasts in a non-stick oven proof sauté pan and place in the oven.
8. Cook for 12 minutes and the turn each breast over.
9. Cook for a further 10 minutes and remove from the oven to a warm plate to rest for 5 minutes.

Chicken and Mushroom Casserole

A comforting casserole topped with soft herby dumplings.

Serves 4

Ingredients

- 500g skinless, boned chicken thighs
- 3 medium carrots, peeled and chopped
- 1 stick celery, washed, halved lengthways and chopped
- 2 banana shallots, peeled and roughly chopped
- 2 cloves garlic finely grated
- 300g chestnut mushrooms, wiped clean, and quartered
- 50ml dry vermouth
- 600ml chicken stock made with 2 stock cubes and boiling water
- 1 bay leaf
- 1 tsp dried oregano
- 1 heaped tbsp plain flour
- freshly ground black pepper
- 1 tbsp crème fraiche
- 2 tbsp olive oil

Dumplings

- 100g self-raising flour
- 50g suet
- 1 tsp dried mixed herbs
- 5 tbsp cold water.

Method

1. Heat oven to 170°C/160°C fan.
2. Trim any excess fat from the thighs, and cut each thigh into two or three pieces (two if small, three if big).
3. Heat the oil in a non-stick sauté pan and brown the chicken in batches. Add them to a casserole dish when browned.
4. Now turn down the heat and gently soften the shallots and garlic by cooking them in the sauté pan in a little oil.
5. Add these to the casserole dish along with the carrots and celery.
6. Sprinkle the flour into the casserole dish and mix well into the ingredients so everything is coated.
7. Add the mushrooms, bay leaf, oregano, some black pepper and again mix well.
8. Deglaze the sauté pan with vermouth.
9. Pour in the hot stock, and add the vermouth from the sauté pan, cover, and cook in the oven for 1.5 hours.
10. Mix together the dry ingredients for the dumplings then add the water a tablespoon at a time and knead into a soft slightly sticky dough. Roll into a sausage shape and divide into eight pieces and roll them into balls.
11. Ladle a small amount of liquid from the casserole into a bowl and whisk in the Crème Fraiche. Mix into the casserole.
12. Increase the oven heat to 200°C/180°C fan. Add the dumplings to the top of the casserole, cover and cook for another 25-30 minutes.

Chicken Escalopes

Tasty, succulent chicken breasts lightly fried in a tangy cheesy crumb.

Serves 4

Ingredients

- 60g panko breadcrumbs
- 25g Parmesan cheese, freshly grated
- 1 lemon, zest only
- 4 chicken breasts, boneless and skinless
- 75g plain flour
- 2 free-range eggs, beaten
- 50g butter
- 1 tbsp olive oil
- sea salt and black pepper
- 1 bunch watercress, leaves picked
- cherry tomatoes
- 1 lemon, cut into wedges

Method

1. Place the breadcrumbs, Parmesan, lemon zest into a food processor and blitz to fine crumbs.
2. Butterfly the chicken breasts (Place the chicken onto what would have been the skin side, then cut down the centre line to half the way through. Turn the knife sideways and cut horizontally almost to the side of the breast to open it out, then repeat with the other side so you have a chicken breast, twice the size it was and half the thickness).

3. Put the flour, crumb and beaten eggs in separate bowls.
4. Season the flour with salt and black pepper then dust the chicken in the flour.
5. Dip into the egg, then into the breadcrumbs, making sure to coat each side thoroughly.
6. Heat the olive oil and the butter in a large frying pan then add the chicken breasts, one at a time, and fry until golden-brown, about two minutes on each side. Place onto kitchen paper to drain.
7. To serve, pile some tomatoes onto the plate, add the chicken and a handful of watercress then finish with a wedge of lemon.

Chicken Marsala

A dash of Marsala wine gives this simple chicken dish a flavour twist. Serve with sweet potato oven chips and steamed green vegetables.

Serves 2

Ingredients

- 2 chicken breasts, skin removed
- 20g plain flour
- 50g butter
- 1 tbsp olive oil
- 1 shallot, finely chopped
- 1 garlic clove, finely grated
- 100g chestnut mushrooms, sliced
- 125ml Marsala (or Madeira)
- 200ml chicken stock
- 100ml double cream
- small handful chopped flatleaf parsley
- salt and freshly ground black pepper

Method

1. Put the chicken breasts between sheets of cling film and beat, using a meat mallet or rolling pin, until about 5mm thick. Season with salt and pepper on both sides.
2. Put the flour on a plate and dip the chicken in it to coat lightly, shaking off any excess.
3. Melt half the butter and oil in a frying pan over medium-high heat and fry the chicken for 2–3 minutes on each

side until golden-brown. Transfer to warm plate, tent with foil and keep warm.
4. Wipe the pan with kitchen paper. Heat the remaining butter and oil over a medium heat and gently fry the shallot and garlic for about 5 minutes until softened.
5. Add the mushrooms and cook for 2 minutes.
6. Add the Marsala and stock and increase the heat to high.
7. Cook until the liquid has reduced in volume by about half.
8. Turn the heat back down to medium, and stir in the cream.
9. Return the chicken back into the sauce. Cook until the sauce thickens (about 3 minutes). Garnish with chopped parsley and serve immediately. (The sauce will continue to thicken off the heat).

Chicken and Sweet Potato Korma

This is a quick and simple to cook curry dish that has lots of creamy, curry flavour and very little chilli heat.

Serves 4

Ingredients

- 2 banana shallots, peeled and sliced
- 2 cloves of garlic, peeled and finely grated
- 1cm ginger peeled and roughly grated
- 2 tbsp of **korma paste** (see recipe on page 138)
- 1 tsp turmeric
- 1 tsp cumin
- 1 tbsp mango chutney
- 4 large boneless, skinless chicken thighs, cut into 2cm pieces
- 2 medium sweet potatoes, peeled and cut into 1cm cubes
- 4 tbsp red lentils (washed).
- 300ml chicken stock
- 400ml coconut milk
- 1 tbsp groundnut oil
- sea salt and black pepper

Method

1. Heat oven to 160°C/150°C fan.
2. Heat the oil in a casserole dish over a medium heat and cook the chicken pieces for 2-3 minutes until they take on a little colour.
3. Now add the shallots, ginger and garlic, stir, and cook for a further 1 minute.

4. Add the korma paste, spices, sweet potatoes, and lentils, and stir until everything is coated, and cook for 2 minutes.
5. Pour the stock, coconut milk and add the mango chutney into the pan, mix well and bring to a simmer. Cover and cook in the oven for 60 minutes, stirring occasionally.
6. Check the seasoning and add salt and pepper as necessary.
7. Serve with steamed green beans and basmati rice or Indian bread.

Chicken Parmigiana

A rich and tasty dish that is easy to cook. Ideal for supper on a cool Autumn evening, served with a pasta of your choice, and a dressed green salad.

Serves 4

Ingredients

- 2 large, skinless chicken breasts, halved through the middle
- 1 egg, beaten
- 75g panko breadcrumbs
- 75g plain flour
- 75g Parmesan cheese grated
- 1 tsp garlic granules

Sauce

- 2 tbsp olive oil
- 2 garlic cloves, finely grated
- 1 banana shallot finely chopped
- 200ml tomato passata
- 200ml chicken stock
- 100g Mascarpone
- 50ml dry vermouth
- 1 tsp caster sugar
- 1 tsp dried oregano
- 1 tbsp fresh basil, finely chopped
- freshly ground salt and black pepper

Method

1. Place the chicken breast pieces between sheets of cling film and flatten to about the thickness of a one pound coin.
2. Add half the Parmesan to the breadcrumbs, the garlic granules if using, and add a pinch of salt and pepper, and mix well.
3. Put the flour, crumb and beaten eggs in separate bowls.
4. Season the flour with salt and black pepper then dust the chicken in the flour.
5. Dip each piece in the beaten egg, and then into the breadcrumbs, and ensure the chicken is completely coated.
6. Place the crumbed chicken on a plate in the fridge whilst you make the sauce.
7. Sauté the shallot in a medium sized pan in 1 tbsp of oil until it is soft, but not browned.
8. Add the garlic, stir and cook for 30 seconds, then add the vermouth, and cook for another minute.
9. Add the passata, stock, sugar and herbs. Mix well, bring to a gentle simmer, and cook for 5 minutes.
10. Now whisk in the Mascarpone, and simmer for two minutes. Check the seasoning and add salt and pepper if required.
11. Heat the oven to 200°C/180°C fan.
12. Heat the remaining oil in a non-stick sauté pan, and lightly brown each piece of crumbed chicken - about 1-2 minutes a side.
13. Place the browned chicken in a layer in the bottom of an oven proof dish and pour the warm sauce over the chicken.
14. Sprinkle the remaining Parmesan cheese over the top and bake in the oven for about 10-12 minutes until the sauce is bubbling and the cheese melted.

Chicken Satay

Tender grilled chicken skewers served with a coconut satay sauce.

Serves 4

Ingredients

Marinade

- 2 large chicken breasts
- 1 tsp lemon juice
- 2 cloves garlic, finely grated
- 1 tsp lemongrass paste.
- 1 cm peeled ginger finely grated
- 2 tbsp dark soy sauce
- a dash of sesame oil
- 1½ tsp groundnut oil
- 1 tsp sweet chilli sauce
- bamboo skewers soaked in water

Sauce

- 4 heaped tbsp crunchy peanut butter
- 100g crushed cashew nuts
- 400ml coconut milk
- 3 tbsp soy sauce
- 1 tbsp runny honey or brown sugar to taste
- Season with pepper

Method

1. Place the chicken breasts between two sheets of cling film and use a rolling pin to flatten them slightly.
2. Remove the cling film and cut the chicken into strips 2.5cm/1 inch wide.
3. Mix together the marinade ingredients and add the chicken - marinade for at least an hour, but no more than 24 hours.
4. Mix the sauce ingredients together in a small pan and gently heat for about 5 minutes until combined.
5. Add the honey or sugar to sweeten if required.
6. Thread one or two pieces of chicken onto each skewer and cook on a barbeque or under a hot grill until golden and cooked through - about 3 or 4 minutes a side. Do not overcook.
7. Serve the skewers with the sauce on the side.

Chicken Tenders

Tasty, succulent chicken breasts baked in a savoury crumb.

Serves 2

Ingredients

- 2 boneless skinless chicken breasts
- 120g mayonnaise
- 2 tbsp Dijon mustard
- 100g panko breadcrumbs
- 1 tsp garlic granules
- 40g grated Parmesan
- sea salt and freshly ground black pepper

Method

1. Chicken tenders are actually the little strips of meat that are loosely attached to the underside of each breast. You can take a boneless, skinless chicken breast and cut it lengthwise into pieces about ½ inch thick and you're left with essentially chicken-tender sized pieces of white meat.
2. Mix the mayonnaise and mustard in a bowl.
3. In another bowl mix panko breadcrumbs, garlic granules, a seasoning of salt and pepper, and about two thirds of the Parmesan.
4. Season the chicken - dip in mayonnaise mix, then in breadcrumbs.
5. Place on a tray and chill in fridge for at least 1 hour.
6. Heat the oven to 200°C/180°C fan. Sprinkle the remaining Parmesan cheese over the tenders and cook for 20 mins on a rack

7. Optional: You can also mix some chopped pistachio nuts or sesame seeds with the breadcrumbs.

Italian Style Buffalo Wings

Serves 4

Ingredients

- 10 chicken wings, cut at the joint into portions

Marinade

- 3 tbsp olive oil
- 2 garlic cloves, finely grated
- 1 tsp dried mixed herbs
- 1 tsp dried oregano
- ½ tsp toasted, ground fennel seeds
- 1 tbsp maple syrup or honey
- sea salt and freshly ground black pepper

Method

1. Mix together the marinade ingredients, add the wings, toss, and marinade in the fridge for at least 2 hours.
2. Heat oven to 200°C/180°C fan.
3. Put a sheet of baking parchment on a tray and place the wings on it. Add any remaining marinade to the wings. Season again with salt.
4. Bake for 15 minutes, remove from the oven, and turn each wing over.
5. Increase the oven temperature to 220°C/200°C fan and bake for another 15-20 minutes until they are golden and crispy.

Hendo's Buffalo Wings

Henderson's Relish is a condiment produced in Sheffield in South Yorkshire, England. It is similar in appearance to Worcestershire sauce, but superior in flavour, and is widely known as "Hendo's". It makes a wonderful addition to these marinated chicken wings.

Serves 4

Ingredients

- 10 chicken wings, cut at the joint into portions

Marinade

- 2 garlic cloves, finely grated
- 2 tsp sweet paprika
- 3 tbsp olive oil
- 2 tbsp Henderson's relish or Worcestershire sauce
- 2 tsp sweet teriyaki sauce
- 1 tbsp honey
- Salt and black pepper.

Method

1. Mix together the marinade ingredients, add the wings, toss, and marinade in the fridge for at least 2 hours.
2. Heat oven to 200°C/180°C fan.
3. Drain and reserve the marinade, then spread the wings out on a baking tray on top of a sheet of baking parchment.
4. Bake for 15 mins.
5. Take out of the oven, turn each winglet over add the reserved marinade, and toss well.

6. Return to the oven and cook for a further 15 mins, tossing a few times to coat (about every 5 mins) in the glaze as they cook. They should be sticky and glazed with most of the marinade evaporated but not burnt. If they look like burning, take them out.
7. Serve on a large platter.

Fish

Fish Cakes

Homemade fish cakes are superior to anything you can buy and are definitely worth the time to make.

Serves 4

Ingredients

- 200g skinned smoked haddock fillet
- 200g skinned haddock fillet
- 150ml milk
- 350g Maris Piper potatoes
- 1 tbsp flatleaf parsley, chopped
- 1 tbsp snipped chives
- 1 heaped tsp mayonnaise
- 1 heaped tsp tartare sauce
- 1 large egg
- flour, for shaping
- 85g panko breadcrumbs
- 3-4 tbsp vegetable or sunflower oil, for shallow frying
- lemon wedges and watercress, to serve
- sea salt and freshly ground black pepper

Method

1. Lay the haddock fillets in a frying pan. Pour over 150ml milk and 150ml water.
2. Bring to a boil, then lower the heat, cover and simmer for 4 minutes. Take off the heat and let stand, covered, for 10 mins to gently finish cooking the fish.
3. Meanwhile, peel and chop the potatoes into even-sized chunks. Put them in a saucepan and just cover with

boiling water. Add a pinch of salt, bring back to the boil and simmer for 10 minutes or until tender, but not broken up.

4. Lift the fish out of the milk with a slotted spoon and put on a plate to cool. Drain the potatoes in a colander and leave for a minute or two.
5. Mash the potatoes with a masher until smooth and beat in the mayonnaise and tartare sauce, chopped flatleaf parsley and snipped chives.
6. Season well with salt and pepper. The potato should have a good flavour, so taste and adjust the seasoning.
7. Drain off liquid from the fish, grind some pepper over it, then flake it into big chunks into the pan of potatoes.
8. Using your hands, gently lift the fish and potatoes together so they just mix. You'll only need a couple of turns, or the fish will break up too much. Put to one side and cool.
9. Beat the egg in a large bowl and lightly flour a plate.
10. Spread the panko breadcrumbs on a plate. Divide the fish cake mixture into four.
11. On the floured plate, and with floured hands, carefully shape into four cakes, about 2.5cm thick. One by one, sit each cake in the egg, and brush over the top and sides so it is completely coated.
12. Sit the cakes on the crumbs, patting the crumbs on the sides and tops so they are lightly covered. Transfer to a plate, cover and chill for 30 mins (or up to a day ahead).
13. Heat 3-4 tbsp vegetable or sunflower oil in a large frying pan.
14. Fry the fish cakes over a medium heat for about 5 mins on each side or until crisp and golden. Serve with the lemon wedges for squeezing over and watercress.

Fish Pie

This sauce thins to a creamy consistency as the fish releases moisture. Baking the fish raw avoids overcooking. You can make the sauce and mashed potato a day ahead and store them, covered, in the fridge.

Serves 6

Ingredients

- 230g haddock fillets, skinless and boneless, cut into 3cm chunks
- 230g salmon fillets, skinless and boneless, cut into 3cm chunks
- 6 large prawns, shelled and chopped in half
- 400g floury potatoes, such as King Edward or Maris Piper, peeled and halved or cut into 5cm chunks
- 40g butter
- 40g plain flour
- 100ml white wine
- 300ml fish stock
- 1 tbsp crème fraîche
- 150ml milk
- 2 tbsp Parmesan, finely grated

Method

1. Put the potatoes in a large pan of cold, salted water and gently bring to the boil. Simmer, uncovered, for 15 to 20 minutes, until tender. Drain, and set aside to steam dry for five minutes. Mash or press through a ricer while still warm. Set aside.

2. Heat the oven to 200°C/180°C fan. In a large non-stick frying pan, melt 50g butter. Add the flour and stir to make a thick paste. Cook over a medium heat for three minutes, stirring.
3. Remove from the heat, then gradually add the wine, stirring until smooth. Return to the heat and add the stock, then bring to the boil and simmer for five minutes, stirring, until the sauce is the consistency of Greek yogurt. Add the crème fraîche. Season and set aside to cool.
4. In a large pan, heat the remaining butter and the milk with plenty of seasoning. Remove from the heat and beat in a third of the mashed potato to a loose consistency, then the remaining potato, until thick and fluffy.
5. Stir the fish and prawns into the sauce. Spoon into a two-litre baking dish. Top with potato, peaking the surface with the back of a fork, then sprinkle on the cheese. Bake for 30 minutes, until golden and bubbling.

Haddock Goujons with a Nut and Herb Crumb

Fish fingers like you've never seen them before... With a crunchy walnut and panko crumb and a hint of Dijon, these goujons will go down a treat. Serve on a platter to share with lemon wedges. This recipe also works well with small fillets of salmon.

Serves 4

Ingredients

- 100g **nut and herb crumb**
- 3 tbsp mayonnaise
- 1 tsp Dijon mustard
- ½ tbsp water
- 500g haddock loin, skinned and cut into fingers
- olive oil spray

Method

1. Heat the oven to 180°C/160°C fan.
2. Place the crumb on a dinner plate.
3. Mix together the mayonnaise and Dijon, then loosen with the water to form a good dipping consistency.
4. Dip the haddock fingers into the mayonnaise mix and then roll in the breadcrumb mixture to coat.
5. Place on a flat baking tray lined with parchment which has been spritzed with 4-5 sprays of olive oil. Spray the goujons with a little oil and place in the oven for about 12-15 minutes (or until cooked through and crispy golden on the outside).

Prawn Cocktail

A simple and elegant Prawn Cocktail recipe.

Serves 4

Ingredients

- lemon juice, to taste
- malt vinegar, to taste
- 20 raw tiger prawns, shells on
- 1 Little Gem lettuce
- 1 sprig fresh thyme, leaves picked
- cayenne pepper, to serve

For the sauce

- ½ lemon, juice only
- 1 tbsp Henderson's Relish
- 5 tbsp tomato ketchup
- a few drops Tabasco sauce (optional)
- ½ tsp paprika
- 1 tbsp double cream
- 4 tbsp mayonnaise
- pinch of sea salt and freshly ground black pepper

Method

1. Bring a large pan of water to the boil and add a squeeze of lemon and glug of vinegar. Add the whole prawns and cook until they rise to the surface. Drain and chill in ice-cold water.
2. Peel the cooled prawns, leaving one prawn whole per serving (for the garnish).

3. Cut the lettuce in half and place in ice-cold water to crisp it up.
4. For the sauce, mix all the sauce ingredients together.
5. To assemble the cocktails, drain the lettuce and pat dry with kitchen paper. Arrange two-thirds of the leaves in four martini glasses or small bowls.
6. Shred the remaining leaves and add to a mixing bowl. Add the peeled prawns and the sauce, and gently mix together.
7. Split the mixture between the bowls and top with the unpeeled prawn and a sprinkling of cayenne pepper.

Salmon with Ginger

A quick and simple, gingery baked salmon supper dish.

Serves 4

Ingredients

- 4 x 125-150g salmon fillets, skin removed

Marinade

- 1 ball of stem ginger chopped onto matchsticks
- 1 tbsp ginger syrup
- 1 tbsp soy sauce
- 1 tbsp dry vermouth
- 1 clove garlic
- Freshly ground Black pepper

Method

1. Mix together the marinade ingredients.
2. Put the salmon in a bowl with the marinade. Cover and chill for 30 minutes.
3. Heat the oven to 200°C/180°C fan. Line a baking sheet with baking parchment.
4. Take the salmon fillets out of the marinade scraping off any bits and pieces and place them on the tray. Spoon some marinade liquid over each piece of salmon. Season with ground black pepper.
5. Bake for 8-10 minutes, depending on the thickness of the salmon.

Tiger Prawn Pasta Sauce

This is a luscious and tasty sauce to pour over your pasta. A side of roasted cherry tomatoes, and a sprinkling of basil and Parmesan cheese rounds off the dish nicely.

Serves 2

Ingredients

- 300g raw tiger prawns, shells removed (keep shells), and leave the tails on 4-6 big ones to use as a garnish
- 1 banana shallot, finely chopped
- 2 cloves of garlic, finely grated
- Optional: small piece of ginger, grated and some chopped fennel
- ½ a small red pepper, finely chopped
- ½ a courgette, cut in half lengthways
- 500ml vegetable or chicken stock
- 3 tbsp crème fraîche
- 1 tbsp tomato puree
- 1 tsp sugar
- splash of vermouth
- olive oil for sautéing
- sea salt and freshly ground black pepper
- pasta of your choice - Tagliatelle is good

Garnish

- Basil leaves, finely sliced
- Parmesan cheese, grated
- 6-8 vine cherry tomatoes

Method

1. Heat oven to 200°C/180°C fan.
2. Run a sharp knife along the back of each prawn and remove the intestinal vein.
3. Add oil to a non-stick sauté pan and gently sauté the shallot and garlic in the oil for about a minute. Do not let them colour.
4. Add the prawn shells, and keep sautéing until they have all turned pink.
5. Add a splash of vermouth and cook for a few seconds to cook off the alcohol.
6. Add the stock, and tomato puree, and bring to a simmer.
7. Simmer for about 20 minutes.
8. Meanwhile put the tomatoes in a small oven proof dish, sprinkle the with oil and salt, and bake in the oven for about 10 minutes. Set aside for use as a garnish.
9. After the sauce has simmered for 20 minutes, taste it. It should be quite "prawny" in flavour. Strain off the stock; put it back in the pan.
10. Reduce it over a medium heat until there is about 300ml of stock left.
11. Whisk in the sugar and crème fraîche and check the seasoning. Keep warm on a low heat. Note: Do not let it boil or the sauce will split.
12. At this point start cooking your pasta.
13. Remove the soft centre of the courgette with a teaspoon, and slice finely - you should have little crescents of courgette.
14. Sauté the courgette and red pepper in a little oil for about a minute.
15. Add the prawns and sauté for a minute or two until cooked. Keep aside the 4 big ones with the tails on for use as a garnish.

16. Add the cooked prawns, courgette, and red pepper mixture to the sauce, and heat through.
17. When the pasta is ready, drain and put into individual bowls. Spoon over the sauce, and garnish with the tomatoes, large prawns, basil and grated Parmesan cheese.

Vegetables

Barley, Butternut Squash, and Spinach Risotto

An excellent vegetarian risotto for a weeknight dinner.

Serves 4

Ingredients

- 1 large banana shallot, finely chopped
- 300g butternut squash, peeled and diced into small chunks
- 2 lumps of frozen spinach leaves, defrosted and squeezed dry
- 2 garlic cloves, crushed
- 1 tsp fresh oregano and thyme, finely chopped
- 1 tsp fennel seeds, toasted and finely crushed
- small glass of white wine
- 100g pearl barley
- 800ml hot chicken stock
- 1 tbsp Mascarpone
- 1 tbsp butter
- 50g Parmesan, grated
- olive oil

Method

1. Heat oven to 200°C/180°C fan.
2. Place the squash chunks in an ovenproof tray, drizzle with oil, and roast in the oven for about 30 minutes, until the squash is cooked and has a good colour. Remove from the oven and leave to cool.

3. Heat the butter in a large shallow saucepan. Add the shallot, and cook very gently, stirring occasionally, until the shallot is soft, about 5 mins. Stir in the garlic and cook for 1 min more. Splash in the white wine and boil down. Add the barley, give it a stir and pour in about 600ml of stock.
4. Add the herbs and fennel seeds, and stir in.
5. Gently simmer for 45 mins, stirring occasionally, until all the stock has been absorbed and the barley is tender. Add a little extra stock during cooking if it evaporates too quickly.
6. Add the cooked squash, and spinach, stir through, and let it warm through for a couple of minutes.
7. Turn off the heat and stir through the Mascarpone, the Parmesan, then season. Spoon into bowls and scatter with extra Parmesan.

Bombay Potatoes

Bombay aloo, otherwise known as Bombay potatoes, is a traditional Indian side dish that uses potatoes boiled, and then spiced.

Serves 4

Ingredients

- 1 thumb-sized piece ginger, grated
- 2 large garlic cloves
- 6 large vine tomatoes, halved, deseeded and chopped
- 800g new potatoes, halved
- 3 tbsp sunflower oil
- 1 large onion, thinly sliced
- 2 green chillies, halved, deseeded and thinly sliced
- 1 tsp black mustard seeds
- 2 tsp ground coriander
- ½ tsp turmeric
- 1 tsp ground cumin
- 2 tsp garam masala
- small bunch coriander, chopped

Method

1. Put the ginger, garlic and four tomatoes into a food processor and blitz until smooth. Set aside.
2. Put the potatoes in a large saucepan. Cover with cold water and bring to a simmer over a medium heat. Cook for 8-10 mins, or until just tender. Drain and leave to steam dry.

3. Meanwhile, heat the oil in a large non-stick frying pan over a medium heat. Add the onions and a large pinch of salt and fry for 15 mins, or until the onions are golden and sticky.
4. Add the chillies, mustard seeds, ground coriander, turmeric, cumin and garam masala to the pan and fry for another 2 mins.
5. Tip in the tomato mixture and bring to a gentle simmer, then carefully stir in the potatoes and remaining tomatoes. Season to taste. Gently simmer the Bombay potatoes for a few mins until everything is warmed through, then serve topped with the coriander.

Boulangère Potatoes

This layered potato dish with onion, and a crispy Parmesan topping, is so named because in France they were given to the local baker to place in a bread oven to cook slowly. Just pop them in the oven where they cook, and then can be kept warm until required.

Serves 4

Ingredients

- 1.5kg Maris Piper potatoes
- 2 onions
- 400ml organic vegetable stock
- 50g Parmesan cheese
- 1 knob of butter

Method

1. Preheat the oven to 180°C/160°C fan.
2. Peel and thinly slice the potatoes, and peel, halve and finely slice the onions.
3. Arrange a layer of sliced potatoes over the base of a 20cm x 30cm baking dish, followed by a layer of sliced onions, and a pinch of sea salt and black pepper. Keep alternating layers of potatoes and onions, lightly seasoning each layer and finishing with a layer of potatoes that slightly overlap each other.
4. Pour over the stock, season the top layer with a little salt and pepper, then scatter over the Parmesan.
5. Put little dots of the butter all over the potatoes, then bake at the top of the oven for 1 hour, or until the top is golden and the potatoes are cooked through.

Dhal

There are many recipes for dhal, but this is the one that I make most often. Serve as a main course with rice or flatbread, or as a side dish to a curry.

Serves 4

Ingredients

- 150g red lentils, washed
- 100g chana dhal, washed
- 1 tsp ground cumin
- 1 tsp turmeric
- 1 tbsp **garam masala** (see recipe on page 135)
- 3 green cardamoms, bruised
- 1 inch of cinnamon stick
- 10 curry leaves
- 1 tbsp brown mustard seeds
- 2 small dried red birds-eye chillies (optional)
- 1 tbsp **ginger and garlic paste** (see recipe on page 136)
- 1 tbsp tomato purée
- 1 large onion cut in half and thinly sliced
- 1 tbsp finely chopped coriander
- 1 litre of vegetable or chicken stock

Method

1. Fry the onions in a little oil until very soft but not browned.
2. Add the ginger and garlic paste and fry with the onions for a minute.

3. Add the spices and stir fry for a minute.
4. Add the stock and mix with the onions and spices.
5. Add the lentils and chana dhal and bring to the boil.
6. Simmer for 25-30 minutes, stirring occasionally to stop the dhal sticking to the bottom.
7. Keep cooking slowly until the chana dhal is tender and the mixture has reached the thickness of dhal required - some folk like it thick and some more like soup.
8. Serve dhal in a bowl.

Extras

- Fry some mustard seeds, cumin seeds, chopped garlic and some small red dried chillies in a tablespoon of oil to make a tarka. When the mustard seeds begin to pop pour the mixture over the dhal in the serving bowl

Spiced Green Lentils

This lentil dish is an excellent accompaniment to grilled meat.

Serves 4

Ingredients

- 150g green lentils, well rinsed
- 1 banana shallot, finely chopped
- 1 small carrot finely chopped
- Half/small stick of celery finely chopped
- 1 medium mushroom, finely chopped
- 500ml chicken stock
- half teaspoon of pomegranate molasses
- 1 tsp honey
- 1 tbsp tomato puree
- 50g dried porcini mushrooms soaked in warm water and finely chopped plus soaking water
- 1 tsp five spice powder
- 1 clove of garlic grated finely
- 1 tbsp olive oil

Method

1. In a medium size saucepan, heat the oil and add the shallots and sauté for about a minute.
2. Add the carrots, celery, and mushroom, stir and sauté for a couple of minutes.
3. Now add the lentils, the stock and the remaining ingredients. Stir well and bring to a simmer.

4. Cook for about 35-40 minutes, stirring every 10 minutes. If it starts getting a bit thick and sticking to the bottom, add a splash of boiling water.

Nut Roast

This is a great vegetarian alternative to the traditional roast dinner.

Serves 4

Ingredients

- 1 large parsnip
- oil, to grease the tin
- 1 small savoy cabbage, 4–6 outer leaves only, or slices of prosciutto (yes, not Veggie!)
- 75g hazelnuts
- 30g butter
- 2 banana shallots, finely chopped
- 75g chestnut mushrooms, finely chopped
- 50g cooked chestnuts, roughly chopped
- 75g Gruyère cheese, grated
- 50g brown breadcrumbs
- 1 tbsp chopped fresh sage
- 1 free-range egg, beaten

Method

1. Peel the parsnips, cut them into quarters (or halves if small) and cook in boiling, salted water until tender, drain thoroughly then mash until smooth.
2. Meanwhile, grease a loaf tin approximately 20cm x 10cm x 7cm, with oil, then line it with foil and grease this generously too. Blanch 6 savoy cabbage leaves in boiling, salted water for 2 mins, until just softened: you'll need enough to line the tin with overlapping leaves, but exactly

how many depends on the size of your cabbage, so make sure you have enough before you tip away the water. Once softened, immediately plunge the leaves into iced water to cool, which will keep them a nice, vibrant green colour.

3. Toast the hazelnuts in a dry frying pan over a high heat until starting to colour, then scoop out and set aside. Turn the heat down to medium, add the butter and chopped onion and cook for 5 mins. Then add the chopped mushrooms and cook for about another 7 mins until the mixture is thoroughly softened.

4. Roughly chop the hazelnuts and put them into a large bowl with the chopped chestnuts, grated Gruyere, breadcrumbs and chopped sage. Add the mashed parsnip, onions and mushrooms, followed by the beaten egg. Season and stir together well so everything is thoroughly combined.

5. Heat the oven to 200°C/180°C fan.

6. Pat the cabbage leaves dry and use to line the prepared tin, leaving any excess leaf hanging over the sides. (Or just line with the prosciutto).

7. Spoon in the mixture, pressing it down well, and fold any overhanging cabbage back over the top to cover. Cover the tin tightly with foil and bake for 45 mins. (Alternatively, you can keep it in the fridge for a day or so at this point, before baking.

8. Remove the foil from the top, put the loaf back in the oven for another 15 mins, until the top is golden, then remove and allow to cool slightly.

9. Put a large serving plate over the top of the tin. Holding the tin securely with oven gloves, turn the plate over so the loaf inverts on to it. Carefully peel off the foil and cut the loaf into slices to serve.

Perfect Mushrooms on Toast

This is one of my favourite lunch dishes.

Serves 2

Ingredients

- 15g butter, plus extra for spreading
- 1 tbsp olive oil
- 300g chestnut mushrooms, wiped clean and halved or quartered
- 1 tsp wholegrain mustard
- 2 tsp crème fraîche or Mascarpone
- A splash of hot water
- thick slices of bread

Method

1. Put the butter in a large frying pan with the olive oil and set over a medium heat. Add the mushrooms, season, then fry for 4-5 minutes, so that the liquid is released, and they start to colour a little.
2. Add a splash of hot water, then stir in the mustard and crème fraîche or Mascarpone.
3. Gently cook for about a minute until heated through, then remove from the heat.
4. Meanwhile, toast the bread. Butter the toast and put on 2 plates. Divide the mushrooms between the toast slices and serve straight away. This is delicious as it is, or with an egg on top if liked.

Pea Soup

An easy light soup ideal for a summer lunch.

Serves 4

Ingredients

- 500ml water
- 1 garlic clove
- 1 medium shallot, finely chopped
- small bunch of basil (or another herb such as parsley or mint)
- 3 tbsp extra-virgin olive oil
- 500g frozen peas
- sea salt and freshly ground black pepper

Method

1. Bring the water to the boil in a pan.
2. Finely chop the garlic, and the shallot, and coarsely chop the herb leaves.
3. Heat 2 tbsp of olive oil in a large-sized saucepan over a medium heat add the garlic, and shallot, and sweat it for 1–2 minutes.
4. Add the peas (still frozen if you wish) and chopped herb leaves and season with a few pinches of salt and a few turns of pepper.
5. Pour in the boiling water. Bring to the boil for 2–3 minutes.
6. Turn off the heat and pour in the rest of the extra-virgin olive oil.

7. With a stick blender, purée the soup to the finest consistency.
8. Taste to check seasoning. Divide the hot pea soup into four bowls and serve.

Risotto Primavera

A great dish for a summer lunch or dinner.

Serves 2

Ingredients

- 1 small garlic clove
- 1 tbsp olive oil
- 800ml good quality chicken or vegetable stock, preferably homemade
- 75g Parmesan or vegetarian alternative, finely grated
- 100ml dry white wine
- 70g shelled peas
- 100g shelled broad beans
- 250g bunch asparagus
- 3 spring onions, trimmed
- 150g risotto rice (Carnaroli or Arborio)
- 2 medium shallots
- 85g butter

Notes

1. As a general rule, 60g rice per person is perfect for a starter, light meal, or if you've bulked out the dish with other ingredients. For more generous portions, go with 75g each.
2. Use hot stock. Whatever type of risotto you're making, use piping hot stock – it means the grains will start to soften and cook straight away. It's a good idea to keep your stock in a covered pan over a very low heat on the back of the hob while the risotto cooks.

Method

1. If using fresh broad beans, drop them into boiling water, leave for 1 min, then drain and cool under cold water. Peel off the skins. For frozen beans, just thaw, then peel.
2. Chop the shallots, spring onions and garlic as finely as you possibly can. Snap the woody bases from the asparagus spears and discard. Slice each spear into 4 diagonal pieces. Pour the stock into a separate pan and bring to a simmer.
3. Heat the oil and half the butter in a heavy, wide pan. Tip in the shallots, spring onions and garlic and cook for 3-4 minutes until soft and see-through, but not brown, stirring often.
4. With the heat on medium, add the rice and keep it moving with a wooden spoon for a few minutes so it gets toasted but not coloured, and very hot. Once it starts to hiss and sizzle, pour in the wine. Keep stirring for about a minute until the wine has evaporated.
5. Put the timer on for 20 minutes (it takes 18-20 minutes to add the stock), now add 1½ ladles of stock, letting it simmer, not boil. Keep stirring until all the liquid is absorbed, scraping the sides of the pan to catch any stray bits of rice. Continue to stir and add a ladleful of stock once the previous amount has been absorbed. (If you add too much stock at a time the risotto won't be as creamy.) The rice tells you when it needs more stock. You will hear it sigh and when you pull a spoon across the bottom of the pan it should leave a clear line.
6. After 14 minutes add the beans and peas to the rice with some seasoning. At the same time, drop the asparagus into the stock and let it simmer for 4 minutes, then lift out with a slotted spoon and add to the rice. Start tasting the rice now too – when done it should be softened, but with a bit of bite in the centre, almost chewy, and the risotto creamy – overcooking just makes it mushy.

7. Continue adding stock and stirring until done (you may have a little stock left). Take the pan off the heat, add half the Parmesan and the rest of the butter plus a splash of stock to keep everything moist. Put the lid on the pan and leave for 3 mins to rest. Serve with the remaining Parmesan.

Stuffed Field Mushrooms

Another great dish for a light lunch or supper.

Serves 2

Ingredients

- 2 field mushrooms
- 1 thick slice of bread, crumbed
- 50 grams red pepper
- 1 garlic clove finely grated
- 50 grams grated Gruyere cheese
- 50 grams chopped walnuts
- 2 spring onions finely chopped
- 1 tsp olive oil
- sea salt and freshly ground white pepper
- ½ tsp mixed herbs

Method

1. Preheat the oven to 180°C/160°C fan.
2. Remove and finely chop the stalks from the mushrooms. Mix in the garlic, spring onion, peppers, nuts, cheese, herbs, and breadcrumbs. Season with black pepper. Finally sprinkle on the oil and use your hands to mix it in well.
3. Spoon the breadcrumb stuffing on and press down lightly. (Do it in a large bowl to catch any spillage).
4. Lay the mushrooms on a non-stick baking tray, stuffing side up.
5. Lay a piece of foil loosely over the top of the mushrooms to prevent the stuffing from browning too quickly and

bake in the oven for 15 minutes. Remove from the oven, discard the foil.

6. Return to the oven and cook for another 10–15 minutes or until the topping is crisp and the mushrooms are tender but not soft. Serve with a large mixed salad.

Stuffed Butternut Squash

A hearty and tasty vegetarian supper dish.

Serves 2

Ingredients

- 1 medium butternut squash, halved length ways and de-seeded
- 3 tbsp olive oil
- 1 large banana shallot, chopped
- 1 large clove garlic, chopped
- 120g basmati rice
- 1 tsp medium curry powder
- 300ml vegetable stock
- 1 dessert apple, cored and grated roughly
- 50g raisins
- 40g toasted pine nuts
- 30g Parmesan (or similar vegetarian hard cheese)
- large handful chopped fresh parsley
- 100g cream cheese with garlic and herbs

Method

1. Heat the oven to 190°C/170°C fan.
2. Using a short, sharp knife and a teaspoon, scrape out a little flesh from each half of squash above where you removed the seeds (leave a 2cm thick edge). This will give you more room for the stuffing. Reserve the flesh and chop.

3. Sprinkle each half of the squash with about 1 tbsp of olive oil and wrap loosely in foil. Place in the oven for 45 minutes or until very soft when pierced with a knife.
4. Meanwhile, a large, heavy based non-stick pan heat the remaining olive oil. Add the shallot and reserved chopped squash and cook for 8-10 minutes until starting to soften and colour.
5. Add the garlic and cook for 1 minute more then stir through the rice and curry powder, mixing everything together well.
6. Add the stock, cover and cook on a low heat for about 12 minutes or until the rice is just cooked.
7. Add the grated apple, raisins, pine nuts, Parmesan and parsley to the rice and stir together, seasoning to taste.
8. Open the foil around the squash halves and divide the rice mixture between them.
9. Dot each half with a tablespoon of the soft cheese.
10. Bake uncovered for 15 minutes then serve with a large salad or steamed vegetables

Baking and Desserts

Bakewell Tart

This tart is lighter than the traditional Bakewell Tart, but just as tasty.

Serves 4

Ingredients

For the short crust pastry

- 120g plain flour
- 60g chilled butter
- 1-2 tbsp cold water

For the filling

- 1 tbsp raspberry jam
- 85g butter
- 85g caster sugar
- 85g ground almonds
- 1 free-range egg, beaten
- ½ tsp almond extract
- 35g flaked almonds

For the icing

- 55g icing sugar
- 1½-2 tsp cold water

Method

1. To make the pastry, measure the flour into a bowl and rub in the butter with your fingertips until the mixture

resembles fine breadcrumbs. Add the water, mixing to form a soft dough.

2. Roll out the dough on a lightly floured work surface and use to line a 15cm flan tin. Leave in the fridge to chill for 30 minutes.
3. Preheat the oven to 200°C/180°C fan.
4. Line the pastry case with foil and fill with baking beans. Bake blind for about 15 minutes, then remove the beans and foil and cook for a further five minutes to dry out the base.
5. For the filling, spread the base of the flan generously with raspberry jam.
6. Melt the butter in a pan, take off the heat and then stir in the sugar. Add ground almonds, egg and almond extract. Pour into the flan tin and sprinkle over the flaked almonds.
7. Bake for about 35 minutes. If the almonds seem to be browning too quickly, cover the tart loosely with foil to prevent them burning.
8. Meanwhile, sift the icing sugar into a bowl. Stir in cold water and transfer to a piping bag.
9. Once you have removed the tart from the oven, pipe the icing over the top, giving an informal zig zag effect.

Brack

Is it a loaf or is it a rich fruit cake? Whatever it is it makes a great teatime treat!

Serves 4

Ingredients

- 350ml cold strong tea
- 200g sultanas
- 150g raisins
- 230g plain flour
- 1 heaped tsp mixed spice
- 2 level tsp baking powder
- 4 level tbsp dark brown soft sugar
- 1 large egg
- butter for greasing the tin

Method

1. Soak the fruit in the tea overnight or at least for a couple of hours.
2. Heat the oven to 180°C/160°C fan.
3. Grease a 1lb loaf tin liberally with butter.
4. Add the flour, baking powder, spice and sugar to a large mixing bowl and stir together, make a well in the centre then break the egg into the well.
5. Add the fruit, which will have soaked up most of the tea, keeping the remaining tea aside, and mix well using a wooden spoon. You should have a wet sticky dough. If it's too dry add some of the reserved tea.

6. Spoon the dough into the prepared loaf tin and bake on the middle shelf of the oven for 50 - 60 minutes. The brack is done when it is a rich golden colour, you can test it by piercing it with a metal skewer, it should come out dry.
7. Leave to cool in the tin for a few minutes then transfer to a cooling rack to cool completely.
8. Wrap in tin foil and keep for 3-4 days.

Carrot and Walnut Muffins

Very easy to make and very moreish!

Serves 4

Ingredients

- 75g butter
- 125g carrots
- 100g sugar
- 100g flour
- ½ tsp cinnamon
- 1 tsp baking powder
- 1 large egg
- 60g sultanas
- 40g walnuts

Method

1. Preheat the oven to 200°C/180°C fan. Melt the butter in the microwave.
2. Top and tail, then peel and grate the carrots.
3. Combine the carrots, sugar and butter in a bowl.
4. Sift in the flour, cinnamon and baking powder.
5. Beat the egg in a small bowl and then add to the mixture. Also mix in the nuts and sultanas.
6. Line a muffin tray with 6 muffin cases and divide the mixture equally between them. Bake for 20-25 minutes.

Christmas Cake

This recipe is based on one created by Mary Berry and is one of the best recipes I have come across.

Serves 8-12

Ingredients

- 175g raisins
- 350g natural glacé cherries, halved, rinsed, and thoroughly dried
- 500g currants
- 350g sultanas
- 150ml brandy or sherry, plus extra for feeding
- 2 oranges, zest only
- 250g butter, softened
- 250g light muscovado sugar
- 4 free-range eggs, at room temperature
- 1 tbsp black treacle
- 75g blanched almonds, chopped
- 250g plain flour
- 1½ tsp mixed spice

For the covering

- 3 tbsp apricot jam, warmed and sieved
- icing sugar
- 700g marzipan

For the royal icing

- 3 free-range eggs, whites only
- 700g icing sugar, sifted

- 3 tsp lemon juice
- 1½ tsp glycerine

Method

1. For the cake, place all the dried fruit, including the cherries, into a large mixing bowl, pour over the brandy and stir in the orange zest. Cover with clingfilm and leave to soak for three days, stirring daily.
2. Grease and line a 23cm deep, round tin with a double layer of greased greaseproof paper. Heat the oven to 140°C/120°C fan.
3. Measure the butter, sugar, eggs, treacle and almonds into a very large bowl and beat well (preferably with an electric mixer). Add the flour and ground spice and mix thoroughly until blended. Stir in the soaked fruit. Spoon into the prepared cake tin and level the surface.
4. Bake in the centre of the oven for about 4-4½ hours, or until the cake feels firm to the touch and is a rich golden brown. Check after two hours, and if the cake is a perfect colour, cover with foil. A skewer inserted into the centre of the cake should come out clean. Leave the cake to cool in the tin.
5. When cool, pierce the cake at intervals with a fine skewer and feed with a little extra brandy. Wrap the completely cold cake in a double layer of greaseproof paper and again in foil and store in a cool place for up to three months, feeding at intervals with more brandy. (Don't remove the lining paper when storing as this helps to keep the cake moist.)
6. The week before you want to serve, begin covering the cake.
7. For the covering, stand the cake upside down, flat side uppermost, on a cake board which is 5cm larger than the size of the cake.

8. Brush the sides and the top of the cake with the warm apricot jam.
9. Liberally dust a work surface with icing sugar and then roll out the marzipan to about 5cm larger than the surface of the cake. Keep moving the marzipan as you roll, checking that it is not sticking to the work surface. Dust the work surface with more icing sugar as necessary.
10. Carefully lift the marzipan over the cake using a rolling pin. Gently level and smooth the top of the paste with the rolling pin, then ease the marzipan down the sides of the cake, smoothing it at the same time. If you are careful, you should be able to cover the cake with no excess marzipan to trim but, if necessary, neatly trim excess marzipan from the base of the cake with a small sharp knife. Cover the cake loosely with baking parchment and leave for a few days to dry out before adding the royal icing.
11. For the royal icing, whisk the egg whites in a large bowl until they become frothy. Mix in the sifted icing sugar a tablespoonful at a time. You can do this with a hand-held electric whisk but keep the speed low.
12. Stir in the lemon juice and glycerine and beat the icing until it is very stiff and white and stands up in peaks.
13. Cover the surface of the icing tightly with clingfilm and keep in a cool place until needed.
14. To ice the cake, place all the icing onto the top of the cake. Spread evenly over the top and sides of the cake with a palette knife. For a snow-peak effect, use a smaller palette knife to rough up the icing.
15. Leave the cake loosely covered overnight for the icing to harden a little, then wrap or store in an airtight container in a cool place until needed.

Granola

This delicious healthy granola recipe is naturally sweetened with maple syrup (or honey). It's made with oats, olive oil and your favourite nuts and fruit.

Serves 8

Ingredients

- 150g rolled oats
- 50g sunflower seeds
- 50g chopped almonds
- 50g chopped pecans
- 50g chopped walnuts
- 50g pumpkin seed
- 50g pistachio nuts
- 75ml olive oil
- 75ml maple syrup or honey
- 1 teaspoon vanilla extract
- 100g mixed dried fruit, sultanas, currants, raisins.

Method

1. Heat oven to 180°C/160°C fan and line a large, rimmed baking tray with baking parchment paper.
2. In a large mixing bowl, combine the oats, nuts and seeds. Stir to blend.
3. Pour in the oil, maple syrup or honey and vanilla. Mix well, until every oat and nut are lightly coated. Pour the granola onto your prepared tray and use a large spoon to spread it in an even layer.

4. Bake until lightly golden, about 20 to 25 minutes, stirring halfway (for extra-clumpy granola, press the stirred granola down with your spatula to create a more even layer). The granola will further crisp up as it cools.
5. Let the granola cool completely, undisturbed (at least 1 hour).
6. Top with the dried fruit (and optional chocolate chips, if using). Break the granola into pieces with your hands if you want to retain big chunks or stir it around with a spoon if you don't want extra-clumpy granola.
7. Store the granola in an airtight container at room temperature for 1 to 2 weeks, or in a sealed freezer bag in the freezer for up to 3 months. The dried fruit can freeze solid, so let it warm to room temperature for 5 to 10 minutes before serving.

Panna Cotta

Panna Cotta is surprisingly simple to make and absolutely delicious.

Serves 4

Ingredients

For the panna cotta

- 2½ platinum grade gelatin leaves
- 150ml milk
- 300ml double cream
- 1 vanilla pod, split lengthways, seeds scraped out or 15ml vanilla paste or 15 ml vanilla extract
- 25g sugar

For the sauce

- 175g sugar
- 175ml water
- splash strawberry liqueur
- 350g strawberries

To serve

- 4 sprigs fresh mint
- icing sugar, to dust

Method

1. For the panna cotta, soak the gelatin leaves in a little cold water until soft.

2. Place the milk, cream, vanilla pod and seeds and sugar into a pan and bring to a simmer. Remove the vanilla pod and discard.
3. Squeeze the water out of the gelatin leaves, then add to the pan and take off the heat. Stir until the gelatin has dissolved.
4. Divide the mixture among four ramekins and leave to cool. Place into the fridge for at least an hour, until set.
5. For the sauce, place the sugar, water and strawberry liqueur into a pan and bring to the boil. Reduce the heat and simmer until the sugar has dissolved.
6. Take the pan off the heat and add half the strawberries. Using a hand blender, blend the sauce until smooth.
7. Pass the sauce through a sieve into a bowl and stir in the remaining fruit.
8. To serve, turn each panna cotta out onto a serving plate. Spoon over the sauce and garnish with a sprig of mint. Dust with icing sugar.

Pear Frangipane Tart

This is a great tart to serve for a party. Always serve it warm.

Serves 8

Ingredients

Pastry

- 100g butter, cut into cubes
- 225g plain flour
- 25g icing sugar, sieved
- 1 egg, beaten

Filling

- 175g soft butter
- 175g caster sugar
- 3 eggs, beaten
- 175g ground almonds
- 40g plain flour
- 1 tsp almond extract
- 8-10 tinned pear halves

To finish

- apricot jam, melted and sieved, for glaze
- 25g flaked almonds, toasted

Method

1. In a food processor, combine the butter, flour and icing sugar in the bowl then process until the mixture resembles ground almonds. Pour in the beaten egg and

pulse the blade until the dough starts to form a ball around the central stem.

2. Form the pastry into a smooth flat cake, wrap in clingfilm and chill for 30 minutes.

3. Make the filling in the unwashed processor. Cream the butter and sugar together, then gradually add the beaten eggs (do not worry if it looks curdled at this stage). Scrape down the sides of the bowl with a spatula. Add the ground almonds, flour and almond extract. Process for a few seconds until well incorporated. Leave this mixture in the fridge until required.

4. Roll out the chilled pastry on a lightly floured work surface and line a flan tin 28cm in diameter, about 2.5cm deep. If possible, chill for a further 30 minutes.

5. Spoon the frangipane mixture into the pastry case and level the top using a small palette knife. Arrange the pear halves, cut side down, attractively on the filling. Be sure to leave enough room between them to allow the frangipane mixture to rise.

6. Heat the oven to 190°C/170°C fan.

7. Put the tin on to a baking sheet and bake for about 45–50 minutes. If the pastry is becoming too dark, place a ring of foil around the edge.

8. Cool slightly, brush with hot apricot glaze and sprinkle with toasted flaked almonds. Serve warm with cream or crème fraîche.

Shortbread

*This is a traditional shortbread which is easy to make. I often serve this with **panna cotta**.*

Serves 4

Ingredients

- 125g butter
- 55g caster sugar, plus extra to finish
- 180g plain flour

Method

1. Heat the oven to 190°C/170°C fan.
2. Beat the butter and the sugar together until smooth.
3. Stir in the flour to get a smooth paste. Turn on to a work surface and gently roll out until the paste is 1cm thick.
4. Cut into rounds or fingers and place onto a baking tray. Sprinkle with caster sugar and chill in the fridge for 20 minutes.
5. Bake in the oven for 15-20 minutes, or until pale golden-brown. Set aside to cool on a wire rack.

Soda Bread

Soda bread is a quick and easy bread to make which uses bicarbonate of soda instead of yeast as a leavening agent.

Serves 4

Ingredients

- 180g plain wholemeal flour
- 180g plain white flour
- ¾ tsp bicarbonate of soda
- ¾ tsp salt
- 300ml buttermilk
- extra flour for dusting

Method

1. Heat the oven to 200°C/180°C fan.
2. In a large bowl, mix together the two types of flour, bicarbonate of soda and salt.
3. Add the buttermilk and mix until a sticky dough forms.
4. Lightly flour a work surface and tip the dough onto it.
5. Gently roll and fold the dough a couple of times to bring the mixture together. Do not knead.
6. Shape the dough into a ball. Flatten the ball gently with your hand. Score the dough with a deep cross dividing it into quarters. Dust the bread with flour.
7. Place onto a baking tray lined with baking parchment and bake for 30 minutes. The loaf should be golden-brown.
8. Leave to cool on a wire rack. This is best eaten on the day of baking.

Sticky Toffee Pudding

Sticky and sumptuous - this recipe is the business! Originally invented at the Sharrow Bay hotel in the Lake District, this dish has become famous all over the world.

Serves 4-6

Ingredients

- 175g golden caster sugar
- 50g unsalted English butter
- 2 large whole free-range eggs
- 200g whole stoned Medjool dates chopped small
- 5g or 1 rounded teaspoon bicarbonate of soda
- 260g freshly kettle boiled water
- 175g self-raising flour
- ½ tsp vanilla extract
- 450g double cream
- 40g black treacle
- 100g dark soft brown sugar
- ¼ tsp vanilla extract.

Method

1. First boil and then weigh the water - weighing is a lot more accurate than using a measuring jug.
2. Carefully add the chopped dates and bi-carbonate of soda (use a large container as the bi-carbonate of soda will make the water fizz up) and leave to soften for around 10 minutes.

3. Using the paddle/beater attachment of your mixer, cream the butter & golden caster sugar until they lighten slightly in colour - approximately 5 minutes.
4. Add the vanilla seeds (or extract if using) and turn the mixer down to its slowest speed.
5. Sift and add the self-raising flour followed at once by the eggs, gradually add the date water mix. Beat for 2 minutes then using a spatula scrape down and gradually increase the mixer speed to around medium until the mixture is evenly mixed (the mixture will be a loose thick pourable batter-like texture-do not be tempted to add any more flour!)
6. Heat oven to 190°C/170°C fan.
7. Pour the mixture into a buttered and floured 20cm x 20cm x 6cm square baking dish and bake for 30-40 minutes - a knife inserted should come out clean.
8. Meanwhile place the double cream, black treacle, de-seeded vanilla pod and dark soft brown sugar in a pan, stirring occasionally, bring to the boil and switch off heat.
9. As soon as your pudding comes out of the oven pour over around half of the toffee sauce onto the pudding (having removed the vanilla pod) and place under a pre-heated grill on highest heat to caramelise the top (or use a blow torch if desired).
10. Serve with the accompanying sauce and a simple vanilla ice cream.

Tiramisu

*The classic, boozy Italian dessert, from **tirami su**, meaning "pick me up" or "cheer me up".*

Serves 6-8

Ingredients

- 100ml strong coffee e.g., espresso
- 4 eggs
- 75g caster sugar
- 450g Mascarpone
- 2 tbsp sweet marsala
- 2 tbsp dark rum
- 16-24 savoiardi biscuits (or boudoir), depending on the size of your dish
- Cocoa powder, to dust

Method

1. Separate the eggs into two large, clean bowls, yolks in one bowl, whites in the other, avoiding contaminating the whites with any yolk.
2. Whisk the whites until they form stiff, rather than droopy peaks – you should be able to hold the bowl upside. Don't over whisk.
3. Beat the egg yolks with the sugar using an electric mixer until voluminous and pale yellow in colour.
4. Drain off any excess liquid from the Mascarpone, if necessary, put it into a bowl and beat with a wooden spoon to loosen a little.
5. Gently beat the cheese into the egg yolks a little at a time, until you have a smooth mixture without any lumps. be

careful not to lose the air whipped into the yolks and sugar.

6. Using a large metal spoon, gently fold a third of the whisked whites into the cheese mixture, then, once that's well combined, fold in the rest, again being careful to knock out as little air from the mix as possible.

7. Put the coffee and alcohol, into a wide dish. Dip each biscuit – savoiardi, are best, because they're drier and lighter than boudoir biscuits or trifle sponges – into the coffee mixture until they're a pale brown colour, and then use them to line the base of a medium serving bowl.

8. Spoon a third of the Mascarpone mixture on top of the biscuits, followed by a generous sprinkle of cocoa.

9. Repeat the layers twice more, finishing with a layer of the cheese mix. Cover and refrigerate for four to six hours before serving, though you can make it a day ahead, if necessary, before ending with a final flourish of cocoa dusted on top.

Walnut and Sultana Bread

The simple addition of walnuts and sultanas to this bread dough transforms an otherwise everyday loaf into something special.

Serves 4

Ingredients

- 300g strong wholemeal flour
- 200g strong white flour
- 8g easy yeast
- 15g salt
- 300g luke-warm water
- 70g sultanas
- 70g walnuts

Method

1. Mix the dry ingredients together in a bowl.
2. Weigh the water and gradually add to the dry ingredients until you have a soft pliable dough.
3. Place the dough on to a lightly floured, flat surface and knead for 10 minutes or use the dough hook of a mixer at speed 1 for 8 minutes. You can tell if the dough is ready by doing the **windowpane test** (see page 142)
4. Put the dough back in the bowl and leave to rise for an hour.
5. Bring the dough out, flatten the dough, and spread the nuts and fruit and roll it Swiss roll style.
6. Shape the dough into a round loaf shape and place on a baking tray. Alternatively split between four mini loaf tins and leave for another 30 minutes.

7. Heat the oven to 200°C/180°C fan.
8. With a sharp knife, cut a line down the centre of the loaf, or mini loaves.
9. Bake for 30 minutes, or until golden brown. Cool on a wire rack.

Sides, Marinades and Sauces

Nut and Herb Crumb for Fish or Chicken

Ingredients

- 30g walnuts
- 30g grated Parmesan cheese
- 1 heaped teaspoon mixed herbs
- 1 tsp garlic granules
- 1 tsp sesame seeds
- 1 tsp crushed toasted fennel seeds
- 40g panko breadcrumbs
- ½ tsp olive oil
- sea salt and freshly ground black pepper

Method

1. Add nuts, sesame, fennel seeds and parsley to a blender and whiz into a rough crumb - don't over whiz.
2. Mix with the panko crumb, Parmesan and garlic granules and add the oil.
3. Season with salt and freshly ground black pepper.

House Gravy Recipe

Ingredients

- 500ml hot water
- 100ml dry vermouth
- 2 good quality stock cubes (chicken, vegetable, lamb or beef)
- 1 shallot, finely chopped
- 1 teaspoon dried oregano
- 2 crushed garlic cloves
- 1 tbsp Henderson's Relish
- 1 bay leaf
- 1 heaped tsp cornflour dissolved in water.
- 1 tbsp olive oil
- pepper for seasoning - you probably won't need salt.

Options:

- Fresh herbs in season, winter savoury, lemon thyme, oregano
- Add a teaspoon of Dijon or grain mustard
- 1 crushed black garlic clove
- Dried tarragon for Chicken or vegetable gravy
- A teaspoon of pomegranate molasses

Method

1. Heat the oil, and gently sauté the chopped shallot.
2. Add in the vermouth and simmer for a minute.
3. Then put everything else, (apart from the cornflour) into a saucepan, bring to a boil and simmer until reduced by about a half.

4. Remove the bay leaf, then use a blender stick, to whizz it smooth.
5. If you have any cooking juices from a roast add these too.
6. If necessary, thicken using the cornflour and water.

Greek Style Marinade

Ingredients

- Handful of fresh herbs, chopped finely (oregano, rosemary, thyme, winter savoury, parsley.)
- 2 large cloves of garlic, peeled and finely grated
- 4 tbsp olive oil
- 1 tsp balsamic vinegar
- 1 tsp honey
- Optional: 1 clove of black garlic, mashed to a paste
- Large pinches of sea salt and freshly ground black pepper

Method

1. Mix all the ingredients together well, and use either as a marinade, or a brushed-on glaze.

Italian Style Marinade

Ingredients

- 4 tbsp olive oil
- 2 garlic cloves, finely grated
- 1 tsp mixed herbs
- 1 tsp oregano
- ½ tsp toasted, ground fennel seeds
- 1 tbsp maple syrup
- 1 tbsp dry vermouth
- Freshly ground black pepper and salt

Method

1. Mix all the ingredients together well, and use either as a marinade, or a brushed-on glaze.

Middle East Style Marinade

Ingredients

- 2 garlic cloves, grated
- 1 tsp sweet paprika
- 2 tsp Za'atar
- 1 tsp **ras el hanout** (see recipe on page 137)
- 2 tbsp olive oil
- 1 tsp balsamic vinegar
- 1 tsp pomegranate molasses
- 1 tsp honey
- Sea salt and black pepper.

Method

1. Mix all the ingredients together well, and use either as a marinade, or a brushed-on glaze.

Inferno Sauce

This will probably be the hottest hot sauce you have ever tasted. I came across this sauce in a small hotel on the island of Tobago where they served it as a condiment with every meal! I eventually persuaded the chef to give me the recipe.

A little goes a long way - it's quite addictive.

Makes about 1.5 litres.

Warning: Do not breathe the fumes when you remove the lid of the food processor.

Ingredients

- 40 Scotch Bonnet chillies, stemmed
- 6 tbsp olive oil
- 20 garlic cloves, peeled and coarsely chopped
- 3 teaspoon molasses
- 50ml honey dissolved in 100ml warm water
- 2 teaspoon turmeric
- juice of 6 fresh limes
- 200ml tomato passata
- 250ml distilled white vinegar
- 2 tbsp salt, or to taste
- 6 tbsp Dijon-style mustard

Method

1. Combine all the ingredients in a food processor and purée until smooth.
2. Correct the seasoning, adding more salt or molasses to taste.

3. Transfer the sauce to clean bottles or jars. You can use it right away, but the flavour will improve if you let it age for a few days.
4. Inferno Hot Sauce will keep almost indefinitely, refrigerated or at room temperature. Just give it a good shake before using.

Pesto

Pesto is a sauce originating in Genoa, the capital city of Liguria, Italy. Ideal for dressing salads.

Ingredients

- 50g pine nuts
- 40g fresh basil
- 50g Parmesan cheese
- 100ml olive oil
- 2 garlic cloves
- sea salt and freshly ground black pepper for seasoning

Method

1. Heat a small frying pan over a low heat. Cook the pine nuts until golden, shaking occasionally. Put into a food processor with the basil, Parmesan, olive oil and garlic cloves. Process until smooth and season.
2. Pour the pesto into a jar and cover with a little extra oil, then seal and store in the fridge for up to two weeks.

Sweet Chilli Sauce

Sweet and hot - goes great with all Asian foods, cold and grilled meat, fish and seafood.

Makes about 1 litre

Ingredients

- 250g fresh red chillies (a medium hot variety)
- 1 tbsp ginger, grated
- 750 ml white vinegar
- 6 cloves garlic
- 2-3 tsp salt, adjust to taste
- 500g sugar
- 300g sultanas

Method

1. De-seed chillies.
2. Place all ingredients in a heavy bottomed pan and simmer until sultanas and chillies are cooked and soft - about 15-20 minutes.
3. Allow to cool. Make a purée in a blender.
4. Store in sterilised bottles.

Tempura

Ingredients

Tempura is a popular Japanese dish of vegetables and seafood coated in a very light and airy batter and fried to perfection.

- 60g cornflour
- 100g self-raising flour
- 1 large free-range egg, yolk only
- 175ml soda water
- sea salt and freshly ground white pepper
- oil for deep frying

Method

1. Pour 4cm of oil into a large wok. Place over a medium heat and heat to 180°C using a cooking thermometer to check the temperature at all times.
2. To make the batter, put the cornflour and, self-raising flour into a large bowl and mix until thoroughly combined.
3. Make a well in the centre. Whisk the egg yolk with half of the water in a separate bowl and gradually add to the flour mixture, using a whisk to draw the dry ingredients into the liquid.
4. When the batter is thick, slowly whisk in the remaining liquid until the batter is just mixed. Don't over-whisk or make the batter too smooth.
5. Drop fish or vegetable pieces into the batter and turn until lightly coated.
6. Working quickly, take one at a time with tongs or a couple of forks and drop gently into the hot oil.

7. Keep the bowl close to your saucepan or fryer as the batter is thin and will drip off quite quickly. Drop into different areas of the pan so that they don't get a chance to stick together.
8. Once all the battered pieces are in the oil, fry for 2–2 ½ minutes, or until pale golden-brown and very crisp. Keep an eye on the temperature of the oil so that it doesn't overheat or cool too far.
9. Use a heat-proof slotted spoon to scoop up any bits of the batter that are left. They should all float as they fry.
10. Remove the tempura with the slotted spoon and drain on kitchen paper.

Velveting

Velveting is a Chinese method of marinating which keeps delicate meat and seafood moist and tender during cooking.

The velveting technique is very easy and gives excellent results. Simply coat strips of chicken, turkey, pork, beef, scallops, or prawns in a mixture of egg white, cornflour, sesame oil and salt before deep-frying in hot oil or stir-frying. The coating creates a protective barrier which seals in the moisture and helps prevent the food from overcooking and becoming tough.

Ingredients

Basic quantity for 2 chicken breasts:

- 1 tbsp whisked egg white
- 2 tsp cornflour
- 2 tsp sesame oil or rice wine
- ¼ tsp table salt

Method

1. Slice the chicken breasts into strips.
2. Mix the ingredients together until smooth and no lumps – the) consistency should be thin.
3. Coat the chicken pieces all over in the batter and leave in the fridge for at least 30 minutes.
4. Then cook briefly in simmering water or hot oil, separating each piece with chopsticks to stop them sticking together. As soon as the pieces turn opaque, but still raw inside (about 40 seconds), lift out and drain.
5. You can then add them to your stir fry once your vegetables or noodles are ready and finish cooking in the

wok for 3-4 mins until fully cooked all the way through and piping hot.

Tips

1. Slicing against the grain shortens the meat fibres which also helps makes meat tender.
2. Some recipes replace the sesame oil with rice wine or rice vinegar.
3. Velveting can be done in advance to save time. It is ideal for stir fries where the vegetables should be cooked separately to the meat according to thickness and texture. Then all ingredients may be brought together at the end, usually tossed with a sauce.
4. Most recipes which call for strips or cubes of meat can be adapted to use this technique before cooking.

Yorkshire pudding

This is a 'no fail' recipe for Yorkshire Puddings - provided you follow the recipe exactly!

Ingredients

- 6-hole muffin tin
- vegetable oil or goose fat
- 2 large free-range eggs
- 100 g plain flour
- 100 ml milk
- good pinch of sea salt and freshly ground white pepper

Method

1. Heat the oven to 220°C/200°C fan.
2. Use a 6-hole muffin tin and add a good teaspoon of oil or fat into each of the 6 compartments.
3. Pop into the oven for 10 to 15 minutes so the oil gets really hot.
4. Meanwhile, sift the flour into a bowl then add the eggs, and milk and a pinch of salt and pepper into the bowl and beat until light and smooth. Then pour the mixture into a jug.
5. Carefully remove the tray from the oven, then confidently pour the batter evenly into the compartments.
6. Turn the oven down to 200°C/180°C fan.
7. Pop the tray back in the oven to cook for 20-25 minutes, or until risen and golden

Spices and Seasonings

Baharat

Baharat is Arabic for "spice", is an all-purpose spice blend widely used in Middle Eastern cuisine. Just a pinch of it adds depth and flavor to sauces, soups, grains, vegetables, stews and meat. I particularly like it in a marinade for lamb.

Ingredients

- 1 tsp ground black pepper
- 1 tbsp ground coriander
- 1 tbsp ground cinnamon
- 1½ tbsp ground cumin
- ½ tsp ground cardamom
- 2 tsp ground nutmeg
- 2 tbsp sweet paprika

Method

1. Mix all the ingredients together. Kept in a small airtight jar, these spice blends will last for 2 months.

Garam Masala

An aromatic spice mix used in many Indian recipes.

Ingredients

Note: *Measures are tablespoons or teaspoons depending on quantity required.*

- 4 ground coriander seed
- 4 ground cumin seed
- 4 ground black peppercorns
- 2 ground green cardamom seed
- 2 ground cloves
- 2 ground mace
- 1 grated nutmeg
- 1 ground cinnamon

Method

1. Dry fry gently (except cinnamon and nutmeg) for 5 minutes, allow to cool and grind all together. Kept in a small airtight jar, this spice blend will last for 2 months.

Ginger and Garlic Paste

This is a staple ingredient of Indian recipes.

Ingredients

- 100g chopped peeled ginger
- 100g chopped peeled garlic
- ground nut oil

Method

1. Add the ginger, garlic and a little oil to a food processor and process until smooth.
2. Add enough extra oil to make a paste.
3. Put in an airtight container, and cover the surface with a thin coating of oil. Will keep in the fridge for about 2 weeks.

Ras el Hanout

The literal translation of ras el hanout from Arabic means "head of the shop" and implies a mixture of the best spices the seller has to offer. There is no definitive composition of spices that makes up ras el hanout. Each shop, company, or family may have their own blend.

Ingredients

- 2 tsp ground ginger
- 2 tsp ground cardamom
- 2 tsp ground mace
- 1 tsp ground cinnamon
- 1 tsp ground allspice
- 1 tsp ground coriander
- 1 tsp ground nutmeg
- 1 tsp ground turmeric
- ½ tsp freshly ground black pepper
- ½ tsp ground white pepper
- ½ tsp ground cayenne pepper
- ¼ tsp ground cloves

Method

1. Mix the spices together. Kept in a small airtight jar, this spice blend will last for 2 months.

Korma Paste

An excellent and flavoursome spice paste for making a very mild curry.

Ingredients

- ¼ tsp cayenne pepper
- 1 tsp garam masala
- 1 tsp ground turmeric
- 2 tbsp ground almonds
- 2 tbsp ground cumin
- 1 tbsp ground coriander
- ½ tsp sea salt
- 2 cloves garlic, peeled and finely grated
- 1 thumb-sized piece fresh root ginger, peeled and finely grated
- 3 tbsp groundnut oil
- 1 tbsp tomato purée

Method

1. Place all ingredients into a food processor and blend to thick paste. If the paste is a little dry, add a tablespoon or so of water and blend again.
2. To store curry paste, transfer to a clean screw-top jar, cover with a layer of oil and keep in the fridge for up to 1 month.
3. To freeze curry paste, spoon into ice-cube trays and freeze. Transfer to a sealable plastic bag and freeze for up to 3 months.

Vegetable Seasoning

Ingredients

A useful mix for seasoning roast vegetables and oven chips.

- 2 tsp sweet paprika
- 2 tsp mixed herbs
- 2 tsp garlic granules
- 2 tsp ground toasted fennel seeds
- salt and freshly ground black pepper

Method

1. Mix all the ingredients together.
2. Put the vegetables into a bowl, sprinkle on the seasoning, then toss to coat well. Sprinkle on some oil, and then toss again.
3. Kept in a small airtight jar, this spice blend will last for 2 months.

Notes and Conversion Tables

Weights and Measures

All weights are in metric - conversion tables are shown below. In the recipes I use 'tsp' and 'tbsp' to represent 'teaspoon' and 'tablespoon', and the measures are rounded not level, unless specifically stated otherwise.

Eggs

All eggs are large size.

Onions

Many of my recipes use echalion (banana) shallots, which I prefer to onions, but you can use ordinary shallots or brown onions instead.

Oils

For general sautéing I use ordinary olive oil (not virgin), and for shallow and deep frying, I use ground nut oil. A good quality vegetable oil can be substituted for both purposes, although the flavour of the dish may not be the same.

Lemons

All lemons should have unwaxed skins.

Flour

Plain flour in the UK is equivalent to North American All-purpose flour. Self-raising flour is sometimes found in the USA - it is plain flour pre-mixed with a rising agent. Strong flour is the UK term for North American Bread flour, and Wholemeal flour is known as Wholewheat in the USA. Flour in the UK tends to be moister than North American flour, so if using North American flour in these recipes, reserve a bit of any liquid used to see if it really needs it.

Meat and Poultry

Wherever possible I use free-range, or outdoor reared meat. Animals that have had a good life and have been well looked after, and preferably sourced from local suppliers and farmers. I am not a supporter of intensive or factory farming. If I cannot get free-range, I will try and get a high welfare product. If I cannot get free-range or high welfare, then I will cook something else instead. I also like to cook Poussins - a Poussin is a young chicken - sometimes called *'coquelet'* - usually between 400–450g in weight. They are very tender and sweet and make very good eating. They are mostly reared in France on specialist high welfare farms.

Vegetables

I also try and source these locally, but inevitably there are some ingredients that are only available as imported products.

Organic

If I can get a good quality organic product, at a reasonable price then I will use it. I don't go out of my way to use organic products, except for carrots. Carrots are more prone to absorbing chemicals than other vegetables, so I always buy organic carrots.

Baking: The Windowpane Test

The windowpane test is one of the best ways to tell if you've sufficiently kneaded your bread dough, though it can sound weird when you come across it in a recipe. Here's how to do it.

First, cut off a small piece of the dough about the size of a golf ball. Hold it between your thumb and first two fingers.

Next, gently spread your fingers and thumbs apart, stretching the dough into a thin translucent membrane (i.e., a windowpane).

If you can stretch the dough without it breaking, that means the gluten is well-developed and your dough is ready to rise. Pat the ball back into the larger batch and you're good ready.

If the dough tears before you've fully extended your fingers, the gluten isn't quite ready yet. Knead the dough for another two minutes and try the windowpane test again.

Liquid Measure Cup, Spoon and Metric

Cup	Metric
¼ cup	60ml
⅓ cup	80ml
½ cup	125ml
1 cup	250ml

Spoon	Metric
¼ teaspoon	1.25ml
½ teaspoon	2.5ml
1 teaspoon	5ml
2 teaspoons	10ml
1 tablespoon (equal to 3 teaspoons)	15ml

Oven Temperatures

Gas Oven Thermostat Setting	Electric Convection Oven °F	Electric Convection Oven °C	Electric fan Oven °C
¼	225	110	90
½	250	130	110-120
1	275	140	120
2	300	150	130-140
3	325	160	140
4	350	180	160
5	375	190	170
6	400	200	180
7	425	220	200
8	450	230	210
9	475	240	220

Printed in Great Britain
by Amazon